Sprawltown

Sprawltown

Looking for the City on its Edges

Richard Ingersoll

Princeton Architectural Press, New York

Published by
Princeton Architectural Press
37 East Seventh Street
New York, New York 10003

For a free catalog of books, call 1.800.722.6657.
Visit our web site at www.papress.com.

Editor: Jennifer N. Thompson
Designer: Deb Wood
Editorial assistance: Lauren Neefe, Lauren Nelson

Special thanks to: Nettie Aljian, Dorothy Ball, Nicola Bednarek,
Janet Behning, Becca Casbon, Penny (Yuen Pik) Chu, Russell
Fernandez, Jan Haux, Clare Jacobson, Mark Lamster, Nancy Eklund
Later, Linda Lee, Katharine Myers, Lauren Nelson, Scott Tennent,
Paul Wagner and Joseph Weston of Princeton Architectural Press
—Kevin C. Lippert, publisher

Library of Congress Cataloging-in-Publication Data
Ingersoll, Richard.
  Sprawltown : looking for the city on its edges / Richard Ingersoll.
    p. cm.
  ISBN-13: 978-1-56898-566-4 (pbk. : alk. paper)
  1. Cities and towns—Growth. 2. City planning. 3. Regional plan-
ning. 4. Urban ecology. I. Title: Looking for the city on its edges.
II. Title.
  HT371.I547 2006
  307.76–dc22
                                        2005026157

Sprawltown
Looking for the City on its Edges

Sprawltown was conceived between Houston, Texas—the mother of all sprawl—and Montevarchi, a small town in Italy. During the period that I was teaching at Rice University, between 1986 and 1997, I also acquired a house in Montevarchi, Italy, where I spent most of my free time. The obvious contrasts and the unexpected similarities between these two places provoked many of the theoretical and historical reflections about urban form and city life that I developed in magazine articles and university courses over the past two decades.

The first essay, "Changing Weather: A New Metaphor for the City," explains the difficulty of understanding and describing the universal condition of sprawl, which has become as much a way of life as a form of urbanism. Sprawl has a certain degree of inevitability due to the incremental growth of populations and the invincible models of consumer culture, and the environmental problems that have grown with it are legion. There is an urgent need to understand urban form and city life through new metaphors in the hopes of recognizing new possibilities of civic value and environmental beauty that can act as the mirrors of human dignity.

"Postcard City: The Symmetry between Tourism and Terrorism," investigates the effects of tourism, currently the single greatest generator of employment and revenue, on urban life. The evolution of the citizen-tourist, incubated in suburban shopping malls but by now present wherever the culture of multinational corporations has taken hold, coincides with the clamorous acts of violence against civilians. The tendency for tourism to transform the real world into simulacra needs to be counteracted by introducing new ways of maintaining a real mixture of productive activities with consumer services for the good of urban vitality and as the self-perpetuating means of security.

In "Jump-cut Urbanism: Cinema, the Automobile, and a New Code of Urban Perception," I claim that the contemporary urban forms that appear scattered and awkward are not as alienating as they might seem if one considers the new codes of perception introduced by the cinematic "jumpcut." Driving a car is somewhat like editing a film. What is missing is the sense of narrative, which is the designer's task.

The new scale of infrastructure imposed by the needs of automobiles has led to an uncanny type of beauty that is not often recognized. In "Infrastructure as Art: Toward Urban Ready-mades," I review the possibilities of finding the beauty in elements such as freeway overpasses and link this to the aesthetic of the sublime in 20th century avant-garde visual culture.

The final chapter, "The Ecology Question: Sprawltown as a Second Nature" is an invitation to consider that the environmental apocalypse, signaled in the discovery of the Ozone holes, Chernobyl, melting polar icecaps, and a myriad of daily climatic instabilities, has already occurred. Rather than being conditioned by guilt-trips or yielding to new forms of eco-fascism, we should rather assume the attitude of cancer patients seeking a way for prolonging life in an agreeable form. No single strategy is sufficient in terms of changing the patterns of resource use and waste of advanced consumer society. In this transitional moment, every act of design should offer new options toward renewable resources. And no technical solution should be conceived outside of a social frame.

Each of the essays is furnished with emblematic illustrations and a series of proactive suggestions based on recent architectural and urban experiences. There can be no pat solutions, nor standard models, only cumulative strategies for rendering the universal condition of Sprawltown more sustainable, civically minded, and beautiful.

Note of thanks

I tried to be comprehensive and objective, but as the great essayist Michel de Montaigne (1580), would have said: "I am the subject of this book." By that I do not mean to imply that my life is so terribly interesting, but rather that I have reached an understanding of things through traveling to places and talking to people. Among my colleagues at Rice were Anderson Todd, Lars Lerup, John Casbarian, Carlos Jimenez, Albert Pope, Sanford Kwinter, Elizabeth Gamard, and Spencer Parsons, and my assistants, Jay Powell, Andrew Cruse, and Larry Albert. Most importantly, Rice introduced me to Stephen Fox, who made the English version of this book more graceful. For five years I served on the board of editors for the Italian magazine Casabella, and in its pages I developed many of these essays. This editorial adventure was guided by Vittorio Gregotti, and assisted by Antonio Angellilo, Bruno Pedretti, Pierre-Alain Croset, Miriam Tosoni, and above all Sebastiano Brandolini, who made the Italian version of this book presentable. I am also grateful to Luis Fernandez Galiano and Adela Garcia, of the Madrid magazine Arquitectura Viva, where I also was given free reign to write about contemporary urban architecture. Kurt Forster, who in the late 1990s was director of the Canadian Centre for Architecture in Montrèal, invited me to organize an exhibition on toy trains, which was important to some of my reflections about infrastructure. Vittorio Magnago Lampugnani invited me to teach a survey in urban history for a year at the ETH in Zurich, which was quite useful for putting my thoughts into a historical perspective. Most of the contents of this book are the basis of a course in urban design that I have developed since 1998 at the Facoltà di Architettura in Ferrara, Italy, where I arrived under the auspices of Paolo Ceccarelli. Maurizio Bonizzi and Nicola Janucci, have been invaluable in developing some of these materials. Since leaving Rice, I have had the good fortune to teach for Syracuse University in Florence, under the leadership of Barbara Deimling and Alick McLean. Others whose work and conversations have been of great influence include Piero Orlandi, Gabriele Basilico, Stefano Boeri, Mirko Zardini, Yung Ho Chang, Paolo

Scrivano, Pippo Ciorra, Marco Massa, Massimo Carmassi, Margaret Crawford, Marco Cenzatti, Cathy Lang Ho, Vittorio Savi, Bernardo Secchi, Paola Viganó, Christophe Girot, Mauro Aurigi e Marco Adriano Perletti. To the late Marco Della Lena, founder of Meltemi publishing house in Rome, I owe the most thanks, since it was due to his insistence that I put the book together. Jennifer Thompson at Princeton Architecture Press has done a superb job in coordinating the English version of the book.

Sprawltown is in some ways the story of my own sprawl to many different places. My wife, Paola Nepi, who is unable to travel, has been the greatest source of wisdom in making sense of what I describe, and to her, my greatest critic, I dedicate the book.

1

Changing Weather
A New Metaphor for the City

Architecture as weather. Blur building,
Swiss Expo 2002, Yverdon, Switzerland,
Diller/Scofidio/Renfro.

Sprawl Is a Way of Life

Almost without notice the city has disappeared. Though people continue to live in places with names like Rome, Paris, New York, and Beijing, the majority of the inhabitants of the developed world live in urban conditions somewhere outside the center city. During the past fifty years, the exponential increase in urbanization has pushed the form of cities beyond the scale of the metropolis to that of the megalopolis: an urbanized territory. The geographer Eugenio Turri (2000) refers to the north of Italy as a single urban phenomenon, with Turin, Genoa, Milan, Bologna, and Venice as high-density points of the *Megalopoli Padana* (The Po Region Megalopolis). The dozen cities studding the Dutch *Randstad* (Rimcity) are lived in as an interurban experience. To speak of "Los Angeles" is to refer to a confederation of forty-two municipalities. The largest conurbation at this time is Tokyo-Yokahama, estimated at thirty-one million residents, and it has close rivals in Asia and Latin America. Can one really call Mexico City a "city" when it includes perhaps twenty-five million people and is more populous than the continent of Australia? And Houston, with a municipal territory of more than six hundred square miles, seems more like a land than a city. All over the world the proportions of cities, both demographically and in area, have exceeded what one is capable of recognizing as a city to become sprawl.

Sprawl was first used by the English in the nineteenth century but has become a particularly American word, introduced during the 1950s to describe the urban growth spilling out from the edges of towns. In European languages there is no satisfactory equivalent. *Periphery, the periurban, conurbations, urban nebulae, exurbia, étalement urbain, la città diffusa,* and *aglomerazión* are all terms that attempt to comprehend a geographical phenomenon that has been repeated in infinite variations during the latter half of the twentieth century, but they fail to convey the intimation of casual and rude demeanor of the original metaphor. *Sprawl* also seems a more appropriate term because it is a verb used as a noun, implying a state of being rather than an actual thing. Although it was once understood as something that occurred on the city's edge, sprawl can now be found between cities and even within the historic districts of a city. And while it initially seemed typical of wealthy societies, it is now the poorer cities, like Cairo and Lima, that are demonstrating the tendency at an alarming pace.

At the end of the nineteenth century, less than ten percent of the world lived in cities. The relationship of a city to its agricultural surroundings was still intact. Today more than fifty percent of the world's population is urbanized, of which sixty percent lives in periurban situations that have displaced crop lands. The distinct categories of urban and rural have become irrelevant (d'Andrea 2000). The equilibrium of city and landscape described in the magnificent fresco *The City of Good Government* in Siena's public palace has been irrevocably upset. Painted by one-time city council member Ambrogio Lorenzetti in 1342, as propaganda, what seemed desirable to fourteenth century republicans was the balance between an architecturally coherent city fabric, free and accessible to all classes, and its supporting agricultural lands, or *contado*. With the recent jumps in scale and segregation of functions and classes, city centers have been hollowed out and fields overrun by development. The center no longer holds one's political or social interest, nor can one any longer have the privilege of seeing what one will eat.

The suffix of my title, *town*, once signified a community of manageable size. During the great urban expansion of the last fifty years, the sense of nearness and direct participation of the town's citizens has been compromised irrevocably by changes in structure and lifestyle. Sprawl can be identified as a geographic and morphological phenomenon that has physically affected the landscape, but it must also be understood as a phenomenon that has triggered anthropological mutations. The civic world of a city square, a main street, or a neighborhood has lost its vitality because, among other things, people no longer live near where they work, nor do they shop where they live, nor do they necessarily desire to live next to each other. The sociable atmosphere of the open market has been sapped of its importance by the convenience of suburban shopping malls. The values of the ancient *polis,* monumentalized in the architecture of the historic centers of Europe and the Americas, have not been reproduced in form or practice in exurban contexts. No-man's-lands prevail as the dominant character of sprawl, and a sense of belonging seems an evanescent condition.

Sprawl continues to grow for many reasons. It was initially attracted to the edges of cities because of cheap land, lower taxes, better access to automobiles, fewer legal restrictions, and the myth of living in contact with rural settings. Although it often seems as if it were spontaneous, it was usually the result of a plan. The incongruities among architectural elements, varying scales, and awkward voids make it seem otherwise. Disorientation has become the norm. The high-speed roads that fragment the exurban landscape lead one to doubt the connection between buildings and streets. One no longer feels that every destination can be reached on foot. Nevertheless, people have adapted to it, and by now the fast cars, billboards, and placelessness of sprawl have become a habit.

Once the scale of the historic city was surpassed, a tendency to experience "community without propinquity," a mode of socialization theorized by Melvin Webber in the 1960s, set in. Social life without nearness can be sustained through various forms of media, in particular through the telephone and Internet. The individual living in sprawl has been liberated from urban space but relegated to a limbo of in-betweenness. One's relation to the city has become more like that of a tourist than of a citizen. Sprawl is thus not just a matter of form but truly a question of a way of life. The philosopher Gianni Vattimo explains this as the typical postmodern condition: "To live in this multiplicitous world means that the feeling of freedom is a continuous oscillation between belonging and estrangement" (Vattimo 1989).

Sprawl first appeared on the margins of cities due to mechanical means of transportation, starting with suburban trains and then automobiles. The economy of petrol and of the automobile has been fundamental to its continued success. At the moment, many exurban ingredients, such as shopping malls and business parks, are being reproduced in center cities. Thus the diffusion of sprawl does not depend so much on positions in space, but on how one moves. All

The periphery of Florence with an Ikea big
box. Looks more like Houston than Italy.

advanced social interactions—work, commerce, culture, health, education, crime, pleasure—are increasingly mediated by electronics. Urban space, which historically served as the conveyor of information, has lost its significance to the superior mobility of cell phones, video, computers, Internet, credit cards, and bar codes. Paul Virilio concludes that "the city is always less a place, less territorial and always more teletopic, profoundly extraterritorial, in which the geometric notions of center and periphery are slowly losing their meaning" (Virilio 1996). To live in sprawl means to find oneself relatively independent of the bonds of space and time.

Sprawltown is an attempt at a synthesis. It is motivated by the desire to find civic values and beauty in situations that have been alienated from any trace of community. I am no longer sufficiently idealistic to believe that one can stop the advance of sprawl, but neither am I so cynical as to think that it is too late to revise certain practices. In the end, sprawl is already a mature form of urbanism, one that by now is in desperate need of restoration.

Sprawl Is Ugly, but Are We Beautiful?

About twenty miles north of the center of Atlanta is an area known by the improbable name of Perimeter Center (1980s). Everything in sprawl tends to be called a "center," yet nothing is truly central. Perimeter Center, a collection of mid-rise towers, shopping malls, and condominium complexes, looks like so many other suburban developments all over America. The paradox of its toponymy is a clear indication that in sprawl a center is not necessarily central and in fact can be completely contradictory to the idea of centrality. Centers can be anywhere because the flows of advanced economies are no longer attached to fixed points. If everything is called "center"—shopping center, sports center, beauty center, business center, convention center—then what can be left for the edge? Franco La Cecla observes that it is the lack of a sense of boundary that is the chief cause of disorientation (La Cecla 1988). The loss of boundaries in a new polycentric exurban environment creates linguistic, if not ontological, anomalies. A "center of the perimeter" perfectly captures the contradictory coordinates of an inscrutable world. You know that you are in the suburbs but can never perceive where you are.

How can one make sense of the conditions and mentalities that produced sprawl? To accurately define the phenomenon is as difficult as predicting the weather. Because of its scale and variety, sprawl defies analytical description. The 1748 Nolli map of Rome, a two-dimensional

Willful disorientation. Perimeter Center, Atlanta, 1990s.

portrait of the city in what has come to be known as "figure-ground" technique, shows the empty spaces of streets, piazzas, and gardens in white, in contrast to the solid hatching of buildings. Such a mode of representation becomes an ineffectual tool when trying to describe an urbanized territory, like the buckshot development surrounding Milan. Seen in figure-ground, the area between Milan and Como seems more like an action painting by Jackson Pollock than urban fabric. The idea of a woven fabric has been undone by the new scale of elevated highways and tall blocks in restructured cities like Beijing. One would have to look to a painter like Alberto Burri, who in the 1950s combined burlap bags with cords and other bits that resemble the shredding and disruption of urban textures. Sprawl needs to be seen in terms of movement rather than in the relations of fixed points. Periurban space is indiscriminately fragmented, and the neat isomorphic relationships between solid and void do not hold: it's either all figure, like the mammoth shopping malls, or all ground, like the endless parking lots. The art of cinematic montage is in fact a better tool of description for the suburbs. Films such as Nicholas Ray's *Rebel Without a Cause* (1955), Federico Fellini's *La dolce vita* (1960), or Jean-Luc Godard's *Deux ou trois choses que je sais d'elle* (1967) opened the discourse about sprawl long before urbanists were able to describe it.

According to the aesthetic criteria of the Renaissance, the pre-industrial city is beautiful and the urbanized areas outside the center are ugly. But one would have to add quickly that there are fragments of historic centers that are horrid and moments of sprawl that are exquisite. The big hole in the ground in the center of Paris now known as Forum les Halles (1970s), where once the lovely ferro-vitreous market sheds of Les Halles stood, is surely a homely replacement. On the other hand, the ever-expanding concrete shells of Charles de Gaulle Airport at Roissy (1980s) offer a sculptural treatment of infrastructure that is of great aesthetic fascination. The beauty of the center can be attributed to its stasis, its space understood according to the vanishing points of perspective, whereas sprawl is always moving, out-of-focus, volatile, and incomprehensible at a glance. There was a time when all cities had a fabric of streets contained in a compact form; the identity of a place and of a community was established by the architectural hierarchy of monuments and urban spaces. While the syntax of street systems and the skylines of various cities were similar, each had its own character and no two were the same. Today the context of sprawl is defined by high-speed roads, elevated interchanges, billboards, and outsize boxy buildings surrounded by parking lots. The same things are repeated many times but without a sense of syntax. Sprawl cannot be read as a unity because one can never grasp it as a whole.

It would be facile to conclude that all suburbs are equal in their apparent disorder just because they reproduce the same scattering of objects: gas stations, warehouses, malls. There is no doubt that European sprawl differs from American; the former tends to maintain a closer connection to the historic center and is always the result of a plan. In some countries, such as Holland and Spain, the plans for the outer edges of cities are scrupulously executed, resulting in a formally coherent fabric. Yet despite their differences, the periurban edges of European cities and Houston are more alike than their respective centers are. To appreciate the seeming chaos of the landscape of sprawl, Henri Bergson's famous dictum regarding physics can still be useful: Disorder is simply an order that we are not yet able to recognize. While this does not excuse the appearance of sprawl, it does offer the possibility that, like the paintings of Pollock, one may some day come to appreciate something that initially seemed incomprehensible. When the day arrives that sprawl begins to make sense, can we anticipate an unleashing of aesthetic and civic resonance?

Within the devastation of the environment caused by sprawl resides the modern project of individual liberty. The sole principle of mass society that has remained unassailable is that everyone should have access to well-being, a dwelling, and work. Universal access to services has become a mandate of modern democracy. In the People's Republic of China it has become a mandate even without democracy. Consumerism, the promise of providing everything to everyone, has transcended politics. Through its myth of individual actualization by way of consumer choices, consumerism has unleashed a rash of wasted resources and environmental damage, leaving a swath of accelerated entropy. The power of consumerism seems unimpeachable, and it is for this reason that sprawl will not let up. In sacrificing the city in pursuit of the illusion of individual liberty, one must ask; *How free are you if you are obliged to use an automobile to go shopping? How can those who are economically better off really feel free if they live in postmodern fortresses?*

If there is a general consensus that sprawl is ugly, can its inhabitants, the beneficiaries of its conveniences, really see themselves as beautiful in this environment? Consumerism proposes that one finds the mirror for a transitory identity in brands and packaging, momentarily satisfying narcissistic desire. Will there come a day when the narcissist discovers that the mirror of life is not really in the objects one consumes, but in the surroundings and social milieu in which one consumes them? To be free to consume is more a form of escape than a path to freedom. Most automobile advertisements emphasize individual empowerment and escape from urban life, but the individualistic flight from an inherited identity preserved in the city is not necessarily liberating. To accept one's responsibility toward others, to take care of the environment, to participate in dialogues that define and resolve collective problems is to negotiate ways of finding freedom, even within the confines of consumerism. The polis was a city based on dialogue. Sprawl is conducive to escapist monologues.

The freedom of the polis was inconceivable without dialogue among equals. Among the practitioners of sprawl, however, the quest for individualistic freedom has led to forms of self-exile, the unconscious punishment of being ostracized from civic life. While one may feel free to escape from the city, there is no way to free oneself from sprawl if it is spreading everywhere. In this respect, all of the alienated fragments of sprawl are waiting for a new awakening of *synoikismos*, the ancient process of agreeing to live together in dialogue. Synoikismos would be a creative tool not just for administrators but for designers as well.

From the Walled Town to the Boundless Urban Territory

In order to talk about sprawl one needs to reassess some of the metaphors that have been used to describe the city. For centuries the "walled town" was understood as a body, completely the opposite of what the scattered urban territory of sprawl seems to be. The speed of contemporary urban life has inadvertently dismembered the corporeal nature of the city. A famous drawing of a city in the shape of a man from the late fifteenth century treatise of Francesco di Giorgio codifies the anthropomorphic ideal of Humanist urbanism: the head is the fortress, the extremities are bastions, the belly is the central piazza, and the heart is the church. Leon Battista Alberti, in his treatise on architecture (1540), used the body metaphor to describe buildings and later suggested that the city is like a house, projecting the notion of familylike social unity. The current dimensions of the metropolis and the disintegration of the family structure, however, detract greatly from the future of this trope.

Another metaphor emerged toward the end of the fifteenth century with the introduction of the military technology of the mobile cannon. Urban theorists produced a more functionalist urban model: the star-shaped, radiocentric city, designed as a war machine. The mechanistic walled city, with angled bastions reached its climax during the sixteenth and seventeenth centuries, with full realizations such as Palmanuova Italy and Neuf Brisack France. The dense, encapsulated fabric of these star-shaped cities was quite the reverse of the gaping holes and stringy patches of today's sprawl.

With the rapid demographic growth and technological transformations of the Industrial Age, the metaphor of the city was inevitably conditioned by the fascination with the factory system. Jeremy Bentham's "panopticon" (proposed in 1791), a radiocentric building ideal for surveying workers in a factory, students in a school, or prisoners in a jail, implied that the city as well could be conceived as an instrument of social control. In the 1770s, C. N. Ledoux's industrial colony at Chaux-les-Salines perfectly anticipated the model, with the central foreman's house providing for the observation of the radial distribution of the workers' housing and factories. The city as a factory was theorized by various social utopians such as Charles Fourier (1830s) and King Gillette (1890s). Fourier's "phalanstery," a project for a single building containing all urban functions for sixteen hundred people, was realized in the 1850s in the factory town of Guise in France, and reprised in Le Corbusier's Unité d'Habitation (1945–56), a twenty-story building isolated in a suburban park for a similar number of inhabitants.

The idea of providing the metropolis with a network of services, including streets, transport, water, sewers, markets, and police, descended from the Positivist line of thought used to organize industrial production. Haussmann in Paris and Cerdá in Barcelona were confident technocrats. The use of scientific criteria regarding hygiene, transportation, and defense led to the unsettling proportions of Parisian boulevards, which were sometimes four to five times the customary width of urban streets. The body metaphor had significantly changed in the seventeenth century after William Harvey's studies of blood circulation and the scientific explanation of how oxygen permeates the organism. During the nineteenth century, the anatomical mechanics of blood and oxygen circulation lent themselves to arterial boulevards and lunglike urban parks. Richard Sennett remarks that the Enlightenment's legacy for urban planning was to conceive of the city in terms of movement rather than in terms of the composition of shaped spaces (Sennett 1998). The new scientific perspective determined the radically open blocks of Cerdá, who proposed leaving up to seventy-five percent of the blocks unbuilt space (in fact, the reverse occurred; much less than twenty-five percent of each block was open space). With the advent of industrial pollution and worker slums, the urban body was often referred to as a sick patient in need of the life-saving interventions of surgeons.

The linear city was a variation of the machine metaphor, corresponding to the engineer's criteria and based on transportation. Arturo Soria y Mata of Madrid produced his model of the "Ciudad Lineal" in 1882, concentrating urban growth in a six-hundred-meter-wide strip of low-density blocks on either side of the tram line. Edgar Chambless's *Roadtown* (1910) proposed a denser version of the linear city as a continuous five-story building, the foundation of which was three layers of train lines stretching from New York to San Francisco. By concentrating development on the infrastructure, one could economize the distribution of services and avoid wasting the agricultural and natural landscapes. In the USSR during the late 1920s and early 1930s the "disurbanist" theory of urbanism, influenced by Nikolai Miliutin, propagated a similar linear-city idea for socialist industrial towns.

Modernist models of urbanism, such as Le Corbusier's Radiant City (1930–35) and Ludwig Hilberseimer's Grossstadt (1927), and a few consonant realizations such as Lucio Costa and Oscar Niemeyer's Brasília (1960) and G. S. Nassuth's Bijlmemeer (1962–71), were based on segregating functions and privileging the lines of circulation of automobiles. The insistence on the primacy of fast roads set up the preconditions for sprawl even in such architecturally coordinated settings.

Christopher Alexander, in his essay "The City is not a Tree," accused the modernists of conceiving their models in overly binary terms, resulting in hierarchical "trees." He notes that in a tree, "no piece of any unit is ever connected to other units, except through the medium of that unit as a whole" (Alexander 1965/1978). This arboreal prejudice led to single-function zoning and the segregation of urban functions. Alexander proposed the "semi-lattice" as a more open and flexible metaphor. His critique anticipated the theoretical distinction of categories made by the philosopher Gilles Deleuze, who wrote of the hierarchical and genealogical tree and its opposite, the non-hierarchical and ahistoric "rhizome" (Deleuze and Guattari 1980). More recently, Albert Pope has demonstrated how both the erosion of the fabric of city centers and the trunk-line organization of the outskirts of cities have transformed urbanism into a series of inflexible "ladders," inhibiting multilateral movement through the urban world (Pope 1996).

One alternative to material metaphors arose in the 1950s with the interest in linguistic models. To propose the city as a language—and

Printed circuits and California cul-de-sacs.

thus to embrace its plurality—was an invitation to abandon architectural solutions and recognize the extent to which the layering of lives created the city. Without making any suggestions for architecture, in 1967 Roland Barthes declared that the city is a language: "We speak our city...simply living it, walking through it and looking at it." Alexander, after his initial attack on modernism, spent ten years producing a manual of architecture with linguistic pretensions: *A Pattern Language*, a system of 253 interactive rules, ranging from the scale of the region to the intimate dimension of one's room (Alexander 1970).

The advent of the computer as a tool and metaphor has consolidated the analogy between language and the city. The complexity of urban factors—topography, geography, hydrology, street systems, voids, buildings, skylines, and so on—is by now completely comprehensible and quantifiable in digital means. Even if the automobile and its needs continue to dominate the organization of the contemporary city, the computer has begun to take over the imagination. Cybercities are now a common experience of childhood in the form of video games. *Simcity* developed in the 1980s was among the first attempts to create a digital conceptualization of the contemporary city in all of its complexity and unsettling fragmentation. In *The Crying of Lot 49* (1966) Thomas Pynchon compares the suburban cul-de-sac subdivisions of California to a computer's printed circuits (Pynchon 1966). The novelist's intuition was quite prescient, as twenty years later personal computers became both a standard ingredient of life in the megalopolis and the greatest means of orientation. When the dimensions of urbanism have become so unfathomable, only the computer is able to guarantee a means of comprehending it and thus a sense of order. The projection of a hybridization of humans and computers into the cyborg will conclude the cycle of metaphors, eliminating through digitized media the factors of space and time, ultimately producing the richness of urban life without the body.

Krierstadt and Generic City

Current urban theories seem to fall into two camps: the "Little City," advocated with evangelical zeal by Leon Krier, and the "Generic City," promoted smugly by Rem Koolhaas. According to Krier, sprawl should be legislated against, and the urban environment should be beautified by returning to the scale and harmony of the pre-industrial metaphor of the body (Krier 1998). The megalopolis and its limitless urban patches can be reconfigured into lots of little cities, each with a central piazza. Instead of scattered body parts, there could be lots of bodies. Koolhaas, on the other hand, describes the city as being irredeemably subject to the flows of advanced capitalism (Koolhaas 1994). Globalism has engendered economic, social, and political forces that, because of their size and complexity, are beyond the control of urbanists and their patrons. The financial interests of multinational corporations and power of consumerism are so strong, markets so domineering, that the collective energies of urbanization resemble a force of nature, like a giant wave. Faced with this sense of inevitability, an architect can react like a surfer confronting the opportunity of the wave. The undulating works of Frank Gehry in Bilbao, Seattle, and Los Angeles may be perfect examples of this maritime metaphor.

Krier grounds his position in the ethnocentric certainty that his corporeal, Little City of Krierstadt—compact and monumental, composed with precise rules governing scale and style—can protect the world from further unseemly development. His aesthetic determinism sustains the rather preposterous notion that if a setting looks like the traditional cities of the past, life there will return to the civic involvement of the *polis*. His proposal is profoundly ideological and would require a political atmosphere of great determination, not to mention autocracy, to be achieved. Koolhaas, on the other hand, in the chaos of the Generic City, recognizes the multicultural urban mosaic that is emerging. The globalization of consumer and producer is an irrepressible force that is destabilizing the coordinates of space and time. His vision is post-ideological and laissez-faire. He reasons that because whatever is repressed will simply pop up someplace else, the idea of legislating design criteria is irrelevant. The profit motive, the great engine of speculation, the habits of waste will continue to produce environments that are undesirable from a social and environmental point of view but clearly satisfactory for transitory consumer desires and short-term amortizations. The guiding axiom for the Generic City: whatever doesn't work should be thrown away. This mode of urbanization, which was generated by marketing surveys without recourse to public responsibility, is cynically utilitarian, ready to appease, its only ethical premise being that it should give pleasure. For the time being, however, it appears that the privileged inhabitants of a presumably civic-minded Krierstadt such as Poundbury in Dorset, England, will probably be obliged to go to work and do their shopping in a nihilistic Generic City, such as Euralille.

How's the Weather?

Since 1985, when the holes in the ozone layer were verified over Antarctica, the weather has become a much more interesting topic of conversation. Global warming, or the "greenhouse effect," is looming as the central political question of the near future. The extreme variations in climate over the past twenty years have been truly alarming, and it is difficult to believe that the causes are not anthropogenic, since the release of carbon dioxide, methane, and other greenhouse gases have increased more than thirty percent from pre-industrial levels. Hurricanes, floods, heat waves, droughts, extreme heat and extreme cold out of season are increasingly common, at escalating cost. The polar ice caps are melting, alpine glaciers are disappearing, and the prognosis that by 2070 the oceans will have risen fifteen inches, causing dramatic changes to coastlines, should be of interest to future Noahs (Godrei 2003).

At the beginning of the new millennium, the weather is no longer a trivial matter. This new sense of political destiny makes climate a fitting metaphor for the current urban situation. Sprawl is a banal phenomenon, just like the weather, and they both have a certain multilateral inevitability. They are even complementary in that urbanization has been accused of being the prime anthropogenic cause in changing the weather. The vast expanses of sprawl reinforce the mass use of automobiles and determine the formidable waste of resources and energy. As long as societal indifference and the constantly changing identity of sprawl continue to elude politicians and professionals, perhaps the most radical thing one can do is attempt to describe what is already an aging form of urbanism.

Even if the weather is nasty, it is not necessarily a negative force, and the same could be said of sprawl. It is doubtful that the current level of well-being in developed countries could have been achieved without it. Reyner Banham, in his famous analysis of Los Angeles, concluded that sprawl is not simply the cause of ecological problems, it is an ecology in itself (Banham 1971). Rather than hopelessly attempting to change the weather, we might start to think meteorologically about its dramatic changes. Though one could sit back and hope the climate improves, it might be best to learn how to exploit what is happening. The natural forces of sun, rain, wind, and geothermic energy, can cause problems but are in fact renewable resources to be studied for their innate power. Climate can be useful in combating changes in the climate.

The ingredients of sprawl, which include tourism, shopping malls, fast cars, freeway interchanges, parking lots, telematic exchanges, single-family houses, and awkward voids, might seem ugly in general, but, by the same logic as "useful" weather, one can recognize good qualities in sprawl, unexpected moments of beauty and civility that can be used as correctives for social and environmental objectives. Although sprawl has produced alienating effects, it should become, by virtue of its predominance, the terrain in which to look toward the possibility of a new social contract. As with the ancient city, which united diverse factions through the process of synoikismos, the fragments of sprawl are waiting for the emergence of a political will to devise strategies for living in this new weather-like condition. Roland Barthes, in his analysis of the collective life of convents, fantasized an urban solution for living together according to the monks' code of "idiorrhythm," whereby all differences are respected and integrated (Barthes 2002). A reckoning with critical weather could finally provide the pretext for a code of idiorrhythm suitable to the near future.

To live well with the weather, one needs to make adjustments and preparations: fix the roof, clear the drains, install the shutters. Sprawltown is a proposal to prepare ourselves for the consequences of the largest urbanization in history. I have attempted to locate areas where communitarian values have survived in spite of sprawl and to propose practices and incentives to improve those areas. Sprawltown is an analytical project intended to stimulate a new urban consciousness amid the vast zones of indifference that abound. One needs, rather than stifle modernity, to complicate its tendency toward mono-functionality and to add other objectives. Infrastructure should not exist just for the sake of expediency, it should become the pretext for art and social welfare. The elements of urbanization can be mixed rather than segregated. Acts of consumption can be reorganized into acts of compensation for the natural world affected by accelerated entropy. Above all, the dweller in Sprawltown desires more options in a world that has been proposed with optimizing criteria.

I have tried in each of the following chapters to assemble some compelling case studies and suggest remedial types of intervention, but I realize that there can be no pat solutions, only strategies. Sprawltown is an invitation to gather under an umbrella and discuss one's place in this changing weather.

2

Postcard City
The Symmetry between Tourism and Terrorism

More tourists than citizens. Venice, Piazza San Marco.

The City as Consumer Good

It is no small irony that the mandate to conserve the image of the historic city is one of the principal factors currently changing urban reality. As the historic city is being frozen in time, preserved, sometimes re-created with mystifications, it is becoming an item of consumption for local amusement and international tourism. This tendency to deploy the "postcard city" under the auspices of promoting historic patrimony is a consequence of the overall commodification of the environment. As hordes of tourists are encouraged to invade historic sites, scrambling impiously about public spaces and monuments, the local populations are either pushed into exile or inducted into meretricious forms of merchandizing. Their possibilities for genuine civic participation are quickly evaporating. The well-intentioned codes of civic pride and hospitality inadvertently help to convert the function of public space from the theater of civic life into a spectacle for tourist gratification. The more that city governments continue to think of urban space as a series of images for mass consumption, both in genuine historic contexts and in new ones, the more they risk compromising the delicate balance between freedom of assembly and free-market exploitation.

The rise of tourism in historic centers—Venice is an extreme case, with fourteen million visitors per year—is literally crushing civic life. The city is being emptied of its productive contents for consumer services. Since the seventeenth century, when Venice was elevated to the playground of the European elite, tourism has exerted a significant economic role. Today it is the principal source of income for the city of floating islands. During the past thirty years, Venice has lost more than half of its residents, passing from 170,000 to less than 75,000. The residents have been driven away by high rents, impractical services, and lack of employment. The coast of the Venetian lagoon, lined with the horrendous petrochemical industries of Marghera and Mestre, has drawn off the working class at great cost to lives and the environment. As sociologist Aldo Bonomi asserts, Venice, the most prominent of world-heritage sites, can be considered a theme park, though much less efficient in managing its profits and services

Fourteen million tourists visit Florence every year.

than Disneyland (Bonomi 2000). The plan for the near future is to charge a visitor's tax to all non-residents upon entering the city, which will in fact complete the transformation of this real place into an ephemeral commodity.

While the effects of tourism are reducing places like Venice to postcard representations, consumer society has promoted the tendency to treat the residents of cities as if they were tourists. When tourism becomes one of the few legitimate uses of urban space, it in fact exerts itself as an ideological question. The tourist, who by definition is remote from the political process of a place and thus is more passive and easier to manage, has become the ideal subject for contemporary urbanism. At the same time that citizens are being displaced by tourists, many cities are attempting to reinforce existing public spaces or to reproduce forms of the historic public realm with touristic criteria. Shopping and spectacle are favored against other forms of civic participation.

Take, for instance, the case of the Piazza della Signoria in Florence. The great L-shaped space that wraps around the public palace evolved during the fourteenth century as the republic's principal space of information. In 1498, when Savonarola met his dramatic end, immolated by papal decree in front of the Palazzo Vecchio, the piazza served as the means of transmitting to the citizenry a profound change in the political situation. Today this same space is engorged with tourists almost year-round, and, despite the fact that the local government still has offices in the palace, the predominant type of information belongs to the global interests of leisure. On the fateful day of September 11th, 2001, I happened to be guiding my American students around this space, when a few of them were alerted by cell phone of the events in Lower Manhattan. We were able to watch the woeful news on a small TV at a corner newsstand. The information and ghastly images of an act of terrorism occurring simultaneously at such a great distance were made immediate in the way Savonarola's execution must have been to fifteenth-century Florentines. Our tour of historic monuments, needless to say, was interrupted by history itself, in the form of the video images of the collapse of the Twin Towers. With regret for the many victims, I was instantly struck by the symmetry between tourism and terrorism.

Why Terrorists Prefer Tourists

Conrad Hilton's seemingly innocuous slogan of the 1950s, "World peace through world travel," has acquired an insidious ideological undertone. It is not tourists who bring peace, of course, but peace that brings tourists. It is difficult, in this regard, to dissociate current practices of global tourism from nineteenth-century imperialism. While tourism may appear to be a peaceful means of redistributing wealth to local destinations, it is no secret that the majority of profits in this sector go to large multinational interests. The statement by the United Nations' World Tourist Organization (WTC) that tourism promotes "international understanding, peace, prosperity, and universal respect for and observance of human rights and fundamental freedom for all" is not that remote from the colonialist ethic of the "white man's burden." In 1841 Thomas Cook founded in London the first tour company, and since then tourism has worked parallel to imperialism, most recently following the multinational system of speculation. The current transnational commodification of leisure includes publicity firms, media corporations, hotel chains, car-rental agencies, tour operators, banks, and airline companies. In general, these profit-seeking agencies have exploited and mystified local cultures without seriously investing in their productive sectors. Already in 1980, in the "Manila Declaration on World Tourism," the imbalance was clearly analyzed: "Tourism does more harm than good to people and societies in the Third World."

More than thirty years ago, Dean MacCannell, in his classic anthropological study, *The Tourist*, observed that international tourism demands the conservation of idealized local cultures, which can be capitalized first as an image of desire and then as a site to sell leisure time. This type of exploitation prohibits the tourist site from evolving or participating in current history and destroys its productive fabric, instituting a parasitic relationship between visitor and resident (MacCannell 1976). As one critic has recently stated:

Tourism is the conspicuous consumption of resources accumulated in secular time; its very possibility, in other words, is securely rooted in the real world of gross political and economic inequalities between nations and classes. In fact...tourism is doubly imperialistic; not only does it make spectacle of the Other, making cultures into consumer items, tourism is also an opiate of the masses in the affluent countries themselves (Crick 1989).

It is not, however, just neo-Marxist intellectuals who identify tourism with imperialism. Unfortunately, tourists have become prime targets for a wide variety of national liberation movements and fundamentalist terror cells. The most spectacular acts of terrorism during the past ten years have frequently been directed toward seemingly innocent tourists. The underlying message seems clear: an attack on international leisure constitutes a blow to imperialism. On July 22, 2003, ETA in Spain planted bombs in tourist hotels in Alicante and Benidorm. A few months earlier, twelve European tourists were kidnapped in Colombia and another five in Algeria. In October 2002, terrorists bombed a discotheque crowded mostly with young Westerners on vacation, killing more than two hundred people. A few months later in Kenya, a hotel for Israeli tourists was torched. In November 1997 in Luxor, Egypt, seventy European tourists were trapped and murdered inside the temple of Queen Hapshetsut, and the year before, a large number of tourists were gunned down in front of the Archaeology Museum in Cairo. Alas, there could be no more prominent tourist attraction than the erstwhile Twin Towers of the World Trade Center in New York (which, even as a gaping ruin, continues to draw tourists). According to Robert Pape, the number of terrorist attacks per year is actually in decline: 348 in 2001 versus 666 in 1987. It is the efficiency of "kamikaze" techniques and the choice of targets that have improved the informational power of terrorism (Pape 2003). The motivations

The luxurious multinational hotels in Cairo.

behind such violence are always political, and the interventions have unfortunately proven to be successful in provoking so-called neo-imperialist nations into vindictive responses, such as the "war on terrorism." Terrorism, with the help of threats of world epidemics of SARS and Avian flu, has had a significant impact on rerouting tourism, driving some airlines into bankruptcy, and, during the past three years, allegedly cutting one in seven jobs in the sector. But consumerism has a notoriously short memory, and there are already indications of recovery published by the World Tourist Organization.

I would not like to give the impression that whoever takes a position against the effects of tourism can be considered a sympathizer with terrorists. Tourism needs to be criticized without placing bombs. In truth, the growth of tourism signifies a huge social victory for democratic societies: the diffusion of general well-being and its attendant leisure time. But free time, just like the time of labor, should be lived conscientiously. A trip to Venice or Katmandu, as a temporary escape from reality, is not necessarily a heinous imperialist act; it just happens to contribute to the cumulative effect of unbalancing the communitarian and productive relations of these settings. To blame the act of tourism in itself would be sheer snobbery, in that both tourists and locals are often satisfied and occasionally illuminated by the encounters it engenders. Rather than condemn tourism as an irresponsible act of international consumerism, one could seek ways of intervening in the reality that attracts tourists, imagining a mode of resistance to gross commodification and civic deterioration.

Esteri

RAFFICHE E BOMBE MOLOTOV: UCCISI 9 TEDESCHI E UN EGIZIANO SUL BUS AL CAIRO

Strage di turisti al museo egizio

Catturati due dei tre terroristi. Gli islamici: «Non sono dei nostri». Ma sparando urlavano: «Infedeli»

Servizio di
Lorenzo Bianchi

Per gli stranieri cinque anni di terrore

Terror attacks on tourists make news in the 1990s.

Two Billion Tourists: The Triumph of Leisure

Tourism is by no means a new factor in world history, it is just that its scale, diffusion, and profitability have recently escalated. In ancient societies, pilgrimages were widely practiced, privileging such places as Delphi, Jerusalem, Mecca, Zimbabwe, Benares, Teotihuacan, and, of course, Rome. The large influx of pilgrims to these cities led to ancillary service industries for food, lodging, tour guides, money changing, entertainment, and prostitution. The income produced from visitors created a type of dependency that conditioned the local economy.

Rome has always had the greatest pull for tourism in Italy. Already in the sixteenth century it had the largest number of hotels per person in Europe. For the 1575 Jubilee year, Rome hosted 400,000 pilgrims (four times the size of its population). One of the main reasons that Rome has never attracted large productive industries is its predominantly service economy, begun around the needs of the Church hierarchy and the influx of its religious faithful and continued with the "grand tour" culture seekers. During the Renaissance the first illustrated guide books appeared, along with *vedute* (topographic prints), which are the prototypes of the postcard. The special private collections of cardinals and nobles became ad hoc museums for the cultural elite, and the cardinals' magnificent gardens, such as Villa d'Este at Tivoli, anticipated the leisure attractions of modern theme parks. The urban renewals of papal Rome—from the first papal axis of Via Alessandrina, built in 1499 between St. Peter's and Castel Sant' Angelo, to the fountains, stairways, and set pieces such as Bernini's colonnade in front of St. Peter's—were earnestly justified as services for pilgrims. *Urbi et Orbi,* "to the city and to the world": the papal government usually directed its public works toward the ephemeral needs of tourism. This perhaps explains why today the city center functions better for visitors than for its working inhabitants, who are eternally frustrated with a circulation better fit for processions than modern traffic.

Notwithstanding historic precedents such as pilgrimages, mass tourism is a modern phenomenon, chronologically in step with the

Pedestrian zone in the historic center of Pienza.
Tourists like to drive to get there and then walk.

expanse of sprawl. It should be noted, however, that the majority of tourist destinations are not cultural, but rather motivated by nature, sports, and places of relaxation. It is nonetheless characteristic of all forms of tourism that the great influx of visitors creates environmental imbalances, social parasitism, and an increase in demand for infrastructure.

It might seem strange to classify something like tourism as an industry, since its products are experiences and images, not tangible consumer goods. Yet tourism has become the world's largest industry, surpassing petrol during the 1990s and employing one in nine jobs worldwide. Its product is literally the environment: cities, mountains, lakes, and beaches. Much like the petroleum industry, which dominated the world economy for most of the twentieth century, tourism achieved its current status in a brief period as an invincible force. It has not so much dethroned petrol as joined forces with it, since mobility is generally the chief expense for the tourist. Almost seventy-five percent of tourists who enter Italy (thirty-nine million visitors in 2003) come by car, fourteen percent by plane, and only eight percent by train. Without gasoline the Italian holiday does not seem possible. The two industries are symbiotically linked and feed each other (Innocenti, 2000).

The paradox that follows is that once the tourist has arrived there is no person on Earth more willing to travel by foot or bicycle. The pedestrian zones in such historic centers as Florence seem geared to the tourists' needs and not those of commercial businesses. Daily life in the pedestrian-friendly zones discriminates against those dependent on the automobile for work-related activities. This inaccessibility has contributed to the emptying of Venice and such other historic centers as Rome, which went from 436,000 inhabitants in the center in 1936 to 137,000 in 1980. While it is impossible to get anywhere on foot in the districts outside the historic centers because of the great distances, in the center it has become impossible to get anywhere by car. Even if one can brave the traffic, the procurement of parking complicates the process. This is one of the reasons that sprawl is so appealing, and it should not go unobserved.

Tourism is thus a service industry that commodifies the environment. It is flexible and multifarious, but, because of its transitory nature, it does not seem to its practitioners to cause serious collateral damage: there are no smokestacks or clouds of pollution. While there are instances of architectural degradation, such as the overbuilding of coastlines with high-rise hotels in warm countries or the multiplication of fast-food joints in historic centers, the greater damage wrought by tourism is a sort of anthropological pollution, which affects the environment through behavior and leisure needs. The tourists, dressed in shorts and baseball caps, looking for fast food in the heart of a historic city, have relaxed the atmosphere and added a somewhat comic element to it; their weight on services, meanwhile the cumulative needs of the two billion tourists who travel annually in the world, is no laughing matter. Tourism affects the management of a city's countless problems with public transport, water, energy, and waste removal.

When German tourists were surveyed, eighty-five percent responded that they would prefer "environmentally friendly" vacations, but for the time being tourism is one of the least environmentally responsible activities. Since the late 1980s, a growing sector of the industry has become known as "eco-tourism," but it has been managed with varying degrees of accountability. If a change in responsibility toward the environment is to occur, it will have to involve not only the conscientious intentions of the individual tourist, but also the guidance of management and politicians. Despite the good intentions of the 1992 Earth Summit in Rio de Janeiro, which resulted in the sustainability policies of Agenda 21, the contradictions of free trade and environmental protection have not been resolved, and the major lobbying societies, such as the World Travel and Tourism Council, prefer that environmental conscientiousness be self-regulatory and not imposed bureaucratically (Honey 1999).

During the past half century, world tourism has leapt from fifty million travelers per year in 1950 to five hundred million in 1980 and more than two billion today. One person in four is a tourist who can afford a vacation. Aside from Italy, which is the fourth largest tourist destination, the major destinations have remained France (seventy-seven million in 2003), Spain (fifty-one million), and the U. S. (forty-one million). The newest arrival to the tourist boom is the People's Republic of China, which became the fifth most popular site during the 1990s (thirty-six million in 2003). During the 1980s the Japanese government, seeking to create a better image of itself in the international trade balance, initiated a program called "Ten million Japanese tourists." From a modest 165,000 tourists in 1965, Japan now sends ten million; notwithstanding the good intentions, it has left a colonial aftertaste. Rather than ingratiating itself to other countries, Japanese tourism is a reminder of that country's economic role (Nicholson-Lord 1997). Cumulatively, 7.6 percent of the world's work force is engaged by tourism, and its income is equal to 10.2 percent of the world's gross product (World Tourist Organization 2004). But these figures do not include the significant shadow economy, or black market, of tourism, which would double these calculated estimates. Thus, just like petroleum in the first half of the twentieth century, tourism for the postindustrial era has become a determining factor that is regularly underestimated. There is a political economy of tourism, similar to that of petroleum, that is latent rather than explicit due to the diffused nature of leisure. To comprehend the political question of tourism, one must consider how it relates to globalism culturally, economically, socially, and politically. One thing is clear: tourism endangers urban identity.

In terms of urbanism, two theories emerge from my analysis concerning the effects of tourism: the first—very reductive—holds that the consumption of an environment, such as a historic city, occurs through simulation, by which the genuine city becomes a perfect and unchangeable copy of itself, the "postcard city." The second—which is inductive—revolves around the conceit that within the parameters of a neo-liberal economy, the ideal citizen is the tourist. This citizen-tourist does not belong to any place in particular, is easily manipulated, and participates in the life of the city mostly through acts of consumerism.

The Tourist Simulacrum: From Old Faithful to San Marino

To illustrate how tourism generates the simulacrum, I would like to make a brief digression from the urban context. About twenty-five years ago, while visiting Yellowstone National Park, I became aware for the first time to what degree tourism was alienating the individual from reality. Amid the vast forests and mountains is Yellowstone's principal tourist attraction, Old Faithful, a geyser that erupts every twenty-three minutes. A semicircular amphitheater of wooden benches had been arranged for viewing the phenomenon, and hundreds of tourists waited patiently with cameras on their knees. At the moment the geyser began spewing, I perceived an orgiastic clatter of camera shutters, several hundred images shot during the first minute. Yet once the photos had been taken, even though the geyser continued to erupt with vigor, the tourists started to leave without any scruples of watching until the end. Old Faithful continued to ejaculate alone for several minutes, and I realized that the simulation obtained through photography had surpassed the full experience of the real. I later learned that a similar conclusion had been reached in more sophisticated terms by Susan Sontag in her book *On Photography* (Sontag 1977).

This tendency to favor the reproduction over the real is clearly present in the historic cities loved by tourists. The constant presence of tourist reproductions eventually converts the authentic situation or artifact into a mystification. MacCannell first identified the process as "staged authenticity," through which the local artifacts, clothing, food, language, and formal aspects of life are reproduced for tourists as unchanging clichés,

Old Faithful, photographed and abandoned, 1978.

suspended in time (MacCannell 1976). That the lace items sold in Bruges are made in China makes no difference to the tourist seeking a ready memento of the city. While the rest of society evolves and changes, the postcard city is embalmed and must remain in its idealized form. Cut off from participation in the real world, it becomes a representation of itself, or, as Jean Baudrillard defined it, a "simulacrum" (Baudrillard 1988).

The Italian hilltop city-state of San Marino, inland from the beach tourism of Rimini's Adriatic coast, offers an extreme case. This micro state of thirty-eight square miles and a population of just under thirty thousand, has over the centuries maintained its political autonomy from the rest of Italy to become a sort of phantom of the medieval past. Its steep outcropping is dotted with three fortresses, which protected the original settlement. Only ten families continue to live in the upper hill town, which has been set aside for the exclusive use of tourists. Below the hill, the modern part of San Marino has grown since the 1950s in a very sprawling manner, with commercial enterprises located on a "strip," public buildings scattered along the main road, and American-style single-family detached dwellings placed in low density on secondary roads. More than most tourist

The Castle of San Marino, Italy, and its suburbs.

cities, San Marino conveys an immediate sense of the tourist simula-crum. It is the favorite destination on rainy days for those who have come to the Adriatic beaches and receives more than four million visitors per year, of whom less than one percent spend the night. Its historic buildings, the fortresses, and the Pieve church (1826–1838) are real historic sites that seem like reproductions. The Palazzo Pubblico (1250–1315) is in fact a notorious fake, rebuilt in the late nineteenth century as an idealized gothic hall. The other medieval buildings are so heavily restored that one is never certain if they are real or have been made over as a movie set.

While the tourists amble about the ramparts, the real population of San Marino lives in the sprawl at the base of this fortified hill, moving mostly by car. Parking in the upper town is not easy, and, despite the fact that citizens of San Marino pay only a token fee for the aerial lift from the lower parking lots to the walled town, there is little reason for them to go there, since both public offices and commercial and productive life have moved to the lower city. Only a few symbolic public functions remain on the hilltop. The wealth of the current inhabitants can be measured by the average of 1.9 automobiles per person! This statistic also explains why the lower

The Castle of San Marino, Italy, and its suburbs.

town, with its wide roads and parking lots, is preferred. Much of San Marino's current economic success came from the development of its eastern edge, where industries and discount commercial enterprises enjoyed favorable tax conditions compared with the rest of Italy. During the 1970s and 1980s, it thrived as a "duty-free" city. While it was sold to tourists with the slogan "Ancient land of liberty," the most notable freedom was from taxes (Stacchini 2003). During the last decade, the city-state, which has a disproportionate number of public employees, has had to initiate steeper sales taxes, approaching those of the rest of Europe. It is still true, however, that the majority of visits to San Marino are not for monuments but for discount shopping. The fortified hilltop shines as an ephemeral presence, hovering above the real city of sprawl at its feet.

This unresolved contradiction between the genuine and the fake, the true city and its tourist double, can be found elsewhere in Italy,

Italia in Miniatura, Little Venice, Rimini, 1990s.

such as Venice, San Gemignano, Capri, and Erice. In most countries where there is a lot of tourism, historic sites are conforming to the trend of the simulacrum and turning into theme parks: Bruges in Belgium, Toledo in Spain, Carcassonne in France, New Orleans in the U.S., Oaxaca in Mexico, and so forth. A few years ago, Francoise Choay caused some controversy by suggesting that the only way to save Venice would be to build a simulation for tourists somewhere else (Choay 1992). In truth, there are already many replicas of Venice—so many, in fact, that when Massimo Cacciari was mayor of Venice, he suggested that the city patent itself and charge copyright fees! At the Venetian hotel in Las Vegas, there is a bit of canal, a Rialto bridge, and a campanile—all fairly bogus imitations. One of the best replicas of Venice—indeed the most charming—is found in the theme park Italia in Miniatura (1970) in the suburbs of Rimini (about two hours south of the real Venice). Perfect replicas of Venetian buildings at five-eighths scale, 120 facades have been modeled in silicon and arranged like stage sets along a forty-centimeter-deep Grand Canal. Connoisseurs will be fascinated by the precision of the imitations of Ca' d'Oro, the Fondaco dei Turchi, Palazzo Grassi, and other famous buildings that did not interest the impresarios of Las Vegas. A sound-track supplies the calls of seagulls and voices from the windows. The seven-minute boat ride ends with a visit to a mini Piazza San Marco (missing the famous pigeons), which does not permit the same sort of intimacy one would have with a real city, but the setting is better maintained and more accessible than today's real version. Nothing can replace the authentic Venice—this is certain—but when the authentic starts to become a simulation of itself, the endless reproduction of an image, the experience of Italia in Miniatura may not be that different.

Choay observed that the appreciation of the facsimile of the caves of Lascaux, Lascaux II, was equal to or perhaps greater than that of the real caves nearby, which have been closed to the general public because the prehistoric paintings are too sensitive to changes in the atmosphere (Choay 1992). The facsimile, or genuine fake, is in fact more legitimate than the mystifications surrounding the original that has been falsified, such as at San Marino. The true fake has a didactic function, is better served by infrastructure, and is usually more environmentally responsible. While this may be true, the complexity of a city like Venice is *not* duplicable. No matter how full of tourists it becomes, one will always find the inspiring grain of civic virtue present in its piecemeal fabric. The real Venice, however, could be partially relieved of the tourist-simulacrum syndrome by shipping some of its tourists to the miniature Venice not far away.

The Shopping Mall:
Incubator of the Citizen-Tourist

At the same time that tourists are displacing citizens, citizens are becoming more like tourists. Consumerism and marketing are quickly converting all practices of self-regulation into forms of management. The shopping mall, which entered the repertoire of architectural types during the 1950s, is the prime site of this anthropological transformation, the incubator of a new social type: the citizen-tourist. The mall idea derived from nineteenth-century urban enclosures, such as the Crystal Palace in London (1851), the Galleria Vittorio Emanuele in Milan (1864), the Galerie Vivienne (1823) and Palais Royale (1783) in Paris, but acquired a completely different urban identity with the automobile. The recent survey of shopping malls by Rem Koolhaas and his collaborators at Harvard proposes that the modern type was spawned by the encounter of the escalator and air-conditioning, but it was the automobile that was the essential catalyst for its success (Koolhaas 2001). A mall is above all an easy place to get to by car and then park.

Despite its origins in European models, the modern mall is a quintessentially American invention, tied closely to the U.S.'s early primacy in mass automobilization. Choice of site for the early shopping malls was conditioned by major nodes of infrastructure and proximity to high-income residential areas (later programs for regional malls required the presence of 250,000 inhabitants within a thirty-mile radius). The shopping centers built in the 1920s and 1930s, such as Country Club Plaza (1922) on the outskirts of Kansas City or Highland Park Village (1931) north of Dallas, had the atmosphere of small-town shops, the difference being their isolation from the city's street system and their provision for twice as much parking as downtown shops (Longstreth 1997).

During the postwar period, the shopping center evolved into the mall type. The early malls, developed in Detroit for Hudson's department store, approached the regional area with a kind of military logic, strategically planting shopping centers, like fortresses, at the four major points of egress on the highways leading toward the city center. The first of these to open was Northland Mall, in 1954, relatively close to the city's wealthiest suburb, Grosse Pointe. Designed by Austrian-born modernist Victor Gruen, who became a sort of Promethean figure in the history of malls, Northland's cluster of buildings was wrapped with an arid band of ten thousand parking spaces. From the exterior it seemed monolithic and impenetrable, but its core focused on a graceful open-air pedestrian concourse, fit with pergolas, flower beds, and benches. The picturesque landscaping was intended to provide a soothing alternative to the harsh city streets of downtown and offer a new possibility for civic space.

Gruen and other mall designers would soon enclose the entire program of the mall, creating a single architectural package, such as Southdale Center in Minneapolis (1956), the central focus of which was a breathtaking, multistoried atrium. The distancing relationship of parking lots, arranged like the vacant *glacis* around a fortress, remained and provided its strongest formal ingredient. While Gruen optimistically proposed this air-conditioned, internalized world, cut off completely from the city, as a new kind of pedestrian-friendly civic space that would eventually attract the mixture of uses of the city, the enclosed malls, privately policed and governed by managers, became in fact the reverse of the civic space (Gladwell 2004). The damage the malls exerted on the civic realm of the downtowns was irreversible. After twenty-five years, suburban malls and exurban businesses had siphoned off more than fifty percent of the retail market. Hudson's, the major client for the first malls in Detroit, was forced to close its downtown department store two decades later, and the sad story of the city's devastated center, while it cannot be attributed directly to the malls, is linked inextricably to this centrifugal exile of retail.

The incubator of the citizen-tourist. Northland Mall by Victor Gruen, Detroit, Michigan, 1954.

The economic success of early shopping centers, usually with at least a seventy percent rate of profit and only a one percent rate of failure, made these projects a deal that could not be resisted. Until the saturation of the market during the 1990s, malls were founded with neither risk nor impunity, creating significant exurban attractors that pulled at the edges of all American cities. There are currently about thirty thousand malls in the U.S., and 2,500 of these are in the regional category, featuring at least two department stores and a hundred shops. There are close to three hundred mega malls, such as the West Edmonton Mall in Alberta, Canada (1981–1998), the Mall of America in Minneapolis (1992), or the Galleria in Houston (expanded 2003), which contain more than a million square feet of retail space. The practice of segregating retail on the edges of cities and exploiting the arteries of fast automobile transit has been repeated with little variation in Europe and Asia, wherever economic and technological, not to mention political, conditions have permitted.

Shopping malls, inasmuch as they are private property, can never become the real public realm, but they sometimes look like it. In many states in the U.S. it is illegal to conduct political activities in privately owned malls, but even in those cities, such as California and New Jersey, where the local courts have upheld the mall's status as a public space, it is quite rare to see any signs of political expression. The separation of functions that has enabled these isolated zones of retail to remain without a connection to the schools, residences, offices, hospitals, and other urban services found in the complex world of the city, has conditioned a new lifestyle: the blasé consumerist demeanor of the citizen-tourist. The time of malls is confined to retail schedules. Security and maintenance are completely in the hands of the management. Those who go to shopping centers become as passive as tourists; they yield their rights of self-determination to a single objective: shopping.

Throughout the 1980s, the success of shopping malls and the astounding decline of city centers—known among planners as the "doughnut effect"—influenced politicians to try to exploit the program of malls as a revitalizing agent for city centers. The novelty was not so much the siting of large shopping centers in the heart of the city, but more in the effort to exploit the historic fabric as a spectacle for shoppers. This new category of mall, the "festival" mall, took root in areas that were slated for renewal. Ghirardelli Square in San Francisco retrofitted the remains of an abandoned chocolate factory in 1964, offering dozens of specialty shops and restaurants with good views of the Bay. It was followed by the much more influential Quincy Market in Boston (1976-78). Adjacent to the latter city's major urban-renewal area (the ill-fated Government Center), the project, designed by Ben Thompson for the Rouse Company, preserved the eighteenth century Faneuil Hall for public functions and retrofitted the nineteenth century market sheds for sixty tourist-oriented shops. The mystique of the historic buildings was united with the lure of consumerism, and the twelve million visitors in its second year of operation outperformed Disneyland. Manhattan got its South Street Seaport (1986), Baltimore its Harbor Place (1978), San Diego its Horton Plaza (1985). Throughout America, the festival mall was welcomed as both a source of economic regeneration and an instrument of social control. The Union Station mall in Washington, D.C., which opened in 1989, is adjacent to crime-filled neigh-

borhoods, the privately policed space, which enforces "good" consumerist behavior, has had a certain sanctuary-like function. In downtowns that had been nearly abandoned, the infusion of shopping-center management completed a phase of social evolution by which local residents became generic citizen-tourists.

A city like Beverly Hills, which never had the intimate scale of narrow historic streets, welcomed at a major intersection of its broad boulevards the Two Rodeo Mall (1990), a curving

A heavily patrolled social life. The Galleria Mall, interior ice-skating rink, Houston, Texas, 1970s.

A street imitating a movie set imitating a street. Two Rodeo Drive by Kaplan McGlaughlin & Diaz, Beverly Hills, California,1980s.

sixteen-foot-wide European-style street. The street was lined with neoclassical facades based on John Nash's London, with street lamps borrowed from Haussmann's Paris, and a cascading stair terminating with a fountain in emulation of baroque Rome. Located not far from the movie studios, Two Rodeo works as a double simulation: an imitation of a movie set in imitation of a European street. It became an instant tourist attraction. The section plan reveals it as a technically clever design in that the slope of the street conceals the three-level parking below, and the change in grade doubles the amount of street-level frontage, which is more commercially valuable.

At the end of the 1980s the success of festival malls in downtown areas and the overdevelopment of malls in the suburbs led to a crisis in the sector, and many malls, after thirty years of activity, were abandoned. One of the first and best-designed malls, Shoppers World (1951), on the edge of Framingham, Massachusetts, which, after its initial bankruptcy in 1952, had successfully served Boston's 128 beltway for forty years, was demolished in the early 1990s despite the efforts of preservationists. Other dead malls underwent cosmetic remakes in the attempt to demonstrate a better urban image. Jon Jerde became a specialist in reworking malls to convey a feeling of urban vitality, creating streetlike scenographies and adding entertainment ingredients to the program. His expertise was required not only in the suburbs of Los Angeles, but also in the rebuilt center of Rotterdam, Netherlands at the Beursplein (mid 1990s).

Jerde's City Walk of the early 1990s, a mall that was commissioned as a propylaeum to Universal Studios' theme park on the northern outskirts of Los Angeles, was intended to simulate the urban experience of city streets, but in the end it seems more like a mall than a street. It nonetheless demonstrates the capacity of shopping environments, with their panoptic systems of control, to pacify potentially dangerous segments of the population. Members of rival gangs that normally terrorize South Central Los Angeles frequently show up at City Walk and are induced to dress and behave appropriately, just like other citizen-tourists. While malls may have contributed to making downtowns less safe and uncivil, there is no doubt that within their hermetically sealed spheres one can feel relatively free of danger. For the elderly, women with small children, and, above all, teenagers, shopping centers signify temporary protection from urban threats. They also, because of climate control, offer a respite from the harshness of adverse temperatures and weather.

The trend to create environments for the citizen-tourist is no longer an exclusively American prerogative. In the seventies, England and France repeated the model, and now there are few European countries without malls. Italy, Germany, Holland, and Spain have during the past ten years opened one or two shopping centers in every large city, usually on periurban sites, causing the same problems for central-city commerce seen in the U.S. during the 1950s. The festival mall would seem to be a strange addition to European cities that already have such strong historic character. Among the first of the genre were Covent Garden Market (1982) and St. Katherine Docks in London (1970s), followed by Forum Les Halles in Paris. Stranger yet are the simulations of historic types in non-urban locations, which have accompanied the latest trend of "designer outlet villages." In Italy, the first of these is Serravalle-Scrivia, in the hinterlands between Milan, Genoa, and Turin. Sited at a five-minute drive from a major node in the autostrada, in an area without other structures,

Designer outlet mall with 250 shops in a simulated historic setting, a huge parking lot, and nothing else. Serravalle-Scrivia, Italy, 2002.

the Serravalle-Scrivia mall (2001) sits stranded like a Potemkin village. Built for an English multinational company with a dozen other such enterprises scattered throughout Europe, the Italian version was designed to reflect its "ethnicity": vaguely rendered in Ligurian style, like the houses at Porto Fino, each of the 150 shops is decorated with upper balconies or fancy windows, plastered in cheerful pastels. The plan weaves three curving streets, which intersect at a large piazza and fountain. Much like Main Street in Disneyland, the facades are in five-eighths scale, thus, the upper stories are not habitable, but only for show. There are no other functions at Serravalle-Scrivia, and outside of 10 A.M. to 8 P.M. it is a completely abandoned place. A safe, village-like environment without the nuisance of villagers, it attracts more than fifty thousand people each week who are eager to find deals on goods that have been discounted from thirty to fifty percent.

Despite the American prototypes, it is still frequent in Europe to find the shopping center combined with other programs. In the suburbs of Madrid, for instance, the Madrid II mall (1986) was developed as part of a civic-center package for the new boulevard Avenida de la Ilustración. A theater, playing fields, and swimming pool were placed adjacent to a conventional mall, its parking confined to an internal garage. An even more interesting combination occurred in Almere, fifty miles east of Amsterdam. The mall was planned in the mid-eighties as a pedestrian node in the urban grid of the city center; stacking offices and housing on its upper stories, it replicated the type of social mix and twenty-four-hour life of the traditional street. In the Bercy district of Paris during the late nineties, the wine warehouses of St. Emilion were converted into a dense network of shops

A new town in Holland with housing and offices above a shopping mall. Almere, 1970s.

and restaurants. Although the project followed to the letter the American formula of festival malls, the urban situation of nearby housing, parks, and offices is so well integrated that the commercial space has been able to sustain the type of civic life that was always present in the city.

The question of obtaining true civic meaning often depends on local administrations to assume responsibility for the realization of shopping environments. In San Antonio, Texas, the River Center, a festival mall built in 1988, resisted some of the alienating effects. Placed between two prime tourist destinations, the Alamo and the Convention Center, it works as a natural pedestrian connector. The developer convinced the city to extend the famous canal system of the River Walk into the project, which was done with the proviso that the outdoor spaces remain public, maintained and policed by the city. For the first time in American mall design, the commercial spaces opened to the street

Mix of public and private. River Center, San Antonio, Texas, 1980s.

rather than being sealed off. Designed by Urban Design Group, of Tulsa, Oklahoma, the extension of the canal was lined with penetrable facades that overlooked the space. People can walk through the mall without feeling they have to consume, and, like the rest of the River Walk, it has become a pleasant part of the city for a promenade.

Another case in which a shopping mall has become a real civic space occurred in Florence, in the suburban district known as Isolotto, where during the 1970s and 1980s the neighbors mobilized to obtain a shopping street and a piazza. Through a public process, the Swiss architect Mario Botta designed a complex that combined the feeling of nineteenth-century covered markets with a small park and a covered piazza. The contours of the street are held down by a long viaduct and a line of poplars. A small park is included on its edge. The parking has been placed in the rear and under the building, far from sight. Along the walls of the triangular covered piazza there are public offices, such as the post office, and the area has become a true node of civic encounter.

An even more complex case of citizen participation occurred in Santa Monica, California, when the four-block, open-air pedestrian mall on Third Street was replanned in the 1990s. In the recuperation effort, the municipality insisted that twenty percent of each of the commercial lots be reserved for housing on the upper levels, some of which had to be low-income and elderly housing. The area, which had been run down and dangerous in previous decades, regained its economic and social viability, as the housing that overlooked the mall gave it a sense of twenty-four-hour security. It is odd that the combination of housing and shopping should seem so original in that until the twentieth century the two had never been separated. The reprogramming of the Third Street mall allowed enough room for the tourist and citizen to mingle together without amalgamating into the hybrid citizen-tourist.

Housing mixed with shopping. Santa Monica Mall, 1990s.

The Museum as Cult Site

When the new wing of the National Gallery in Washington, D.C., opened in 1976, its similarity to a shopping mall was instantly clear to all. The same was said about the renewed MoMA in New York in the 1980s. This equivocation of cultural into commercial types was an effect not only of the large atrium space, which had become the iconographic element of the mall, but also of the way the museum experience was structured to mix the viewing of works of art with activities such as shopping, eating in a nice restaurant, and going to a film. Even the renewed Louvre in Paris by I.M. Pei (1989) demonstrates this symbiosis of shopping and art: while the prominent glass pyramid serves as the new entrance, an inverted glass pyramid a hundred yards north of it brings daylight to an underground concourse of elegant shops, which lead from the Metro stop to the foyer. Andy Warhol made his career on the ambiguity of art and commerce by recycling the advertising icons of consumer culture, and this same ambiguity is now found at an institutional level in the major museums of the world. In Rotterdam, the Kunsthal (1992), a museum of contemporary art designed by Rem Koolhaas, plays explicitly with this conceit by situating a billboard as the vertical element of its massing; the device alternates genuine commercial messages with information on the exhibitions.

As a program, the museum has become a last refuge for high-style architecture. According to Kenneth Frampton, the more tawdry and uninhabitable the urban environment becomes, the more the museum is set apart as a reserve of civility and beauty (*Design Book Review* 1986). It is as if the museum were a scapegoat for the ravages of sprawl. Frank Gehry's Guggenheim Bilbao illustrates how a museum can come to represent a city the way cathedrals once had the power to signify. During its first year of operation in 1998, more than a million tourists came to see it, transforming the identity of Bilbao, which had until then been an industrial port city without tourism. While the recent Guggenheim's success is probably unrepeatable, the lesson seems clear: the museum is a strategic marketing tool for a city.

Waiting for the "Bilbao Effect." Bellevue Art Museum by Steven Holl, Washington, 2001.

The "Bilbao effect" has been sought by many municipal administrations in the hope of entering into the mythos of global tourism. A new museum, The Vesunna Gallo-Roman Museum devoted to Roman antiquities in Périgueux, a provincial city in southwest France, was commissioned from Jean Nouvel (an architect whose work always generates media attention) in 1993 and finished in 2002. Despite its aesthetic appeal, however, tourism has not significantly increased. The museum is beautifully conceived and full of genuine treasures, but Périgueux is not well connected to the rest of the world. A similar process occurred in Bellevue, a city on the edge of Seattle, where Steven Holl was commissioned to design Bellevue Art Museum (2000), a museum of contemporary art, in an area full of shopping malls and office parks. After only three years of activity the museum went bankrupt, and, although the director identified Holl's overly mannered architecture as the problem, one must ask whether any architectural solution could have performed better in such an alienated situation.

The museum as a marketing device reached its apex in Frankfurt in the 1980s. Nine museums were built in the span of ten years in the rebuilt city center, which was devastated

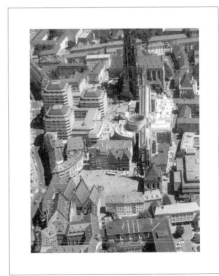

The Shirn district's reconstructed center as museum and cultural center. Frankfurt, Germany, 1980s.

during World War II. It is as if the city collected museums like artworks: a Richard Meier, a Hans Hollein, a Matthias Ungers.... A similar attempt at a collecting strategy occurred in San Francisco during the same period, with a new museum of modern art by Mario Botta, an arts center by Fumihiko Maki, a civic auditorium by James Stuart Polshek, and gardens by Mitchell/Giurgola. Both in Frankfurt and San Francisco, the impression made by so many cultural institutions grouped together has been a bit like that of the monofunctional shopping center, which brings many stores together in relative isolation. These museum enclaves risk transmitting a sort of mall narcosis and, instead of renewing civic life, become places for citizen-tourists, incapable of inspiring a sense of belonging to a civic environment.

To avoid the numbing experience of museums, the programs should include more aspects of daily life. Centre Pompidou in Paris, designed by Richard Rogers and Renzo Piano (1971–76), is probably the most transgressive museum of the twentieth century in following the challenge launched in the 1960s by the French minister of culture, André Malraux, who imagined a museum without walls. Its erector-set image conveys the sense of a building that is changeable and constantly in process. The program included France's first open-stack library, a mediatheque, exhibition spaces, a film center, a bookstore, and a restaurant. The great innovation was nevertheless the large, sloping exterior piazza and the equally large interior piazza, which became instant gathering places for all social classes. (Since the increase in terror threats in the 1980s, however, it has been more stringently controlled, and clochards are no longer allowed.) Being located in the center of Paris, of course, contributed to its success, but the openness and mixture of its functions have made it the single most popular arts institution in the world.

Copying the program of Centre Pompidou, the city of Nîmes in southern France achieved a similar success in the 1990s, commissioning Norman Foster through a competition to design the Carrée d'Art. Placed next to the ancient Roman temple, the Maison Carrée, the new cultural center has become an integral part of the city, as much enjoyed by tourists as local citizens. Almost the reverse of the Roman building, which is a compact mass with a small dark interior, the new building creates a neutral screen, mediating the climate and serving as a backdrop for the ancient temple. Inside it opens to two lower stories and three upper ones, all naturally lit. People come to read the newspaper, see videos, consult the library, and go to exhibitions. The ascent to the restaurant on the roof offers an incomparable panoramic view of the city.

Perhaps the most extraordinary example of how a museum can become an agent of resistance and restore a sense of civic belonging occurred in the privately funded Menil Collection in Houston, designed by Renzo Piano (1982–87). The patron, Dominique de Menil, a French emigrée, had for more than thirty years been influencing artistic taste in what was a resolutely backwater city. She chose a residential neighborhood adjacent to a small university, within walking distance of the city's Museum of Fine Arts but far from downtown. During the 1970s, she and her husband had sponsored the Rothko Chapel (1971), which became an ecumenical institution for the city of Houston. Before beginning construction on the museum, which was to house an eclectic collection of more than twenty thousand works, ranging from surrealism to abstract expressionism to ethnic arts, the patron acquired all the adjacent bungalow houses in a six-block area and uniformly painted them gray with white trim. Once the museum was constructed, it was energized by the presence of the little houses, where artists, poets, and other members of the cultural community have been able to rent space. Some of the houses are used for the museum's offices, such as for

A productive community for art. Menil Collection by Renzo Piano, Houston, Texas, 1986.

the Image of the Black documentation project. Inside the museum, admission to which is free, there are no commercial activities, not even the chance to buy a postcard; one may only be involved with the works. The form of the museum is anti-monumental, horizontal, surrounded by graceful white porticoes of steel H-columns that hold up ferro-cement louvers for shade. The parking lot is located on an outer block, not directly on axis to the entry, and visitors feel a clean break with the world of traffic as they enter the slowpaced precinct of the museum. While visiting the top-lit galleries, one becomes aware of people intervening on artworks by peering obliquely into the restoration studio at the end of the corridor; and as one circum- ambulates the building's porticoes, the activity of cultural workers in the bungalows conveys the sense of a productive community rather than a temple of consumerism. In a city where no one walks, the porticoes surrounding the museum have become a favorite itinerary for promenades. The Menil Collection and its bungalows make one aware that the subject of the museum is no longer a passive art appre- ciaton, but now a creative process with a deeper connection to art.

Cities Without People:
Las Colinas and Milano Due

Most American downtowns are deserted after 6 P.M., while most residential areas show little sign of life from nine to five. In many cases, the center city is only for offices and tourism, while shopping centers are full of citizen-tourists. In all cases, the real citizens, the ones who feel they belong to a place, the ones who feel they have the right to complain when they disagree with public policy, are disappearing, partly because of social evolution and partly because of economic and political choices. The prevailing impression in the conditions of sprawl is that the city is without people.

The open spaces, once the leisure grounds of the entire community, have frequently been abandoned, falling into disrepair, sometimes occupied by bands of delinquents, homeless, and other socially marginlized types. The choice of living away from the central city is often a flight from perceived urban threats, dangers that increased the moment the city was segregated by function, class, and race. Public safety and social control were traditionally maintained by the constant presence of citizens in an urban environment that was inhabited by a variety of classes twenty-four hours a day. Once the flight from the center begins, it is impossible to reconstitute a cohesive network of citizens. Personal safety becomes a major factor, if not *the* major factor, in the dwelling choices of the new bourgeoisie. During the past thirty years, various forms of gated communities, enclaves protected by walls, checkpoints, and private guards have proliferated on the edges of cities. Currently an estimated eight million Americans live in such situations, and the number is growing (Blakely and Snyder 1997). The edges of Houston, Atlanta, and Los Angeles, not to mention of Rome and Madrid, contain dozens of gated communities, ruled with unquestioned authority by development managers. There is perhaps a sense of belonging in such places, but it can only be as meaningful as a membership to a country club.

The emergence of the city without people can be seen in the cases of two extremely successful real-estate ventures: Las Colinas, near

The ultimate bourgeois utopia. Las Colinas, Dallas, Texas, 1980s.

Dallas, Texas, and Milano Due, near Milan, Italy. Both were begun in the early 1970s as attempts to create residential enclaves for the new bourgeoisie. Neither is within the limits of the center city, where taxes and services are more expensive and legislation more strict. Las Colinas comprises forty square miles, planned for a hundred thousand residents. The developer, Ben Carpenter, made his fortune in insurance and transformed his ranch property, which is closer to the Dallas–Fort Worth airport than to downtown Dallas, into a master-planned development. Organized by the young Silvio Berlusconi (who subsequently became the wealthiest Italian alive as well as the country's prime minister), Milano Due was a much smaller project. It too is closer to an airport (Linate) than to the center city.

Each of these enclaves resorts to the strategy of using the nodes of highway infrastructure as a desired advantage; in the case of Las Colinas, the publicly funded freeway that runs through it was named after the developer. Before his bankruptcy, Carpenter's corporate offices were located in the central skyscraper of the so-called Urban Center, overlooking the fountain on Williams Square (named after his brother-in-law). Berlusconi's offices for Fininvest and one of his TV stations, Canale 5, are located in the tallest building of Milano Due, and overlook the pond. Both of these developments are isolated and cut off from contiguous urbanization by natural features and arterial thoroughfares.

Las Colinas was planned as a refuge for the corporate rich, from the dangers and inefficiencies of the central city. About a third of the land was developed for office towers and business parks, so that the executives could live close to where they work. It hosts one hundred corporate headquarters, eighty multinational companies, and five hundred high-tech firms. The price of real estate in Las Colinas has guaranteed that there are no poor residents, and the buffer of woods and college campuses at its edges has insulated it from the possibility of infiltration from the poorer areas beyond its boundaries. The houses are grouped on closed-circuit roads in gated clusters. Although there is no sense of connection from one cluster to the next, the houses are all connected to a centralized electronic surveillance system. The roads of Las Colinas are wide and curvilinear, with staggered intersections designed to avoid the need for traffic lights. Golf courses separate residential areas from business zones, and it is nearly impossible to walk from a place of residence to a place of work, since there are no connected pathways.

A dozen skyscrapers fifteen to thirty stories in height have been built in the Urban Center,

A tourist village for everyday life. Milano Due, Italy, 1980s (plan below).

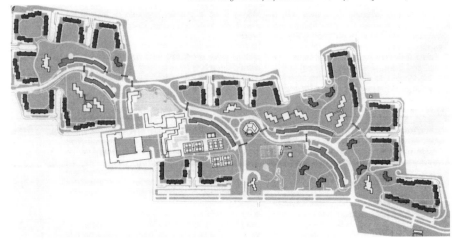

each with a multilevel garage. A lake that gathers the rain runoff fills the voided core of the Urban Center, while to one side, wedged between the parking garages, a hundred-foot pedestrian canal, lined with incongruous arcaded facades borrowed from Mexican architecture, has been inserted in emulation of Venice. Speedboats driven by Venetian-style gondoliers await tourists. Parallel to the canal, a monorail, worthy of a World Expo, was built as a horizontal elevator to connect the high-rises, but was only in operation for a few years before going out of service. At the base of the major cluster of towers is Williams Square, which is based on the dimensions of Trafalgar Square in London. A diagonally placed fountain with colossal mustangs, that seem to be galloping due to the squirts placed at their hooves, was intended as a point of gathering; except for the tourists, however, the plaza is rarely occupied. Those who work in the buildings park in the rear garages and have no need to cross the plaza to get to their offices. The piazza, the canal, and the lake of Las Colinas have become tourist attractions in a city that has only one other competing venue, the Sixth Floor, near the site of the John F. Kennedy assassination.

The residents of Las Colinas are automatically considered members of a homeowners' association, which establishes the rules of behavior and to which one pays a monthly fee to insure protection and maintenance. To be a citizen of Las Colinas is to be a member of a club, but the political decisions are in the hands of the development managers. Even though it seems like an independent town, Las Colinas is officially under the jurisdiction of Irving, a town just outside the Dallas city limits. The taxes and political questions are thus simplified so that one can live as a citizen-tourist, apart from the problems of a real city, in this ultimate bourgeois utopia.

A similar atmosphere of a vacation resort infuses Milano Due. It is located in the city of Segrate, which is tangent to the edge of Milan but not beholden to its stricter codes. Berlusconi developed more than a thousand apartments as the cornerstone of a financial empire that now includes seventy percent of the Italian media. The area and population of Milano Due are less than ten percent of Las Colinas, but in the Italian context it represents one of the most cohesively executed privately initiated master-planned developments. It is structured on a single curving street that, like the roads of Las Colinas, avoids the need for traffic lights by staggering the intersections. The picturesque atmosphere is achieved by lining the street with steep, grassy berms, which create a noise barrier while craftily concealing the ground-level garages that serve the apartments. All of the minor streets are closed-circuit roads. Pedestrian circulation has been carefully separated from that of cars by jacking it up to the second level and making connections across the main artery over Venetian-style footbridges. While there are no barriers or checkpoints in Milano Due, it gives the impression of a segregated enclave, and safety is guaranteed by the presence of a private police force, which constantly patrols the grounds. The apartments are stacked in five-story structures with pitched tile roofs and generous balconies. The views look onto landscaped interior parkland, in which there are tennis courts, swimming pools, and cultural facilities. Some of the apartment buildings have connecting porticoes at the pedestrian level with the provision for two dozen shops, but only a few of the commercial businesses have been able to survive. For the inhabitants of Las Colinas and Milano Due, shopping is an activity to be carried out via automobile and usually in a designated center.

As at Las Colinas, the central landscape feature of Milano Due is a lake. In this case, with its jet-like fountain similar to the one in Geneva, the lake has become the iconic representation of Canale 5. On the northern shore of the lake is the only real "public" space in the development: a small, irregularly shaped piazza with three restaurants, benches, and pergolas—an impoverished version of Portofino. Much like Las Colinas, the parking for the offices that look onto this piazza is located on the other side of the buildings, so that it is not necessary to cross the public space to get to the work place. The piazza comes to life briefly around 12:30 P.M., when workers start to go on their lunch break, but never gives the impression of gathering a crowd. It will never become political space, except in the sense of condoning the considerable interests of the developer. Despite the attempt to replicate public space, all of the internal spaces of Milano Due are private, and the armed guards, paid for through monthly condominium fees, quickly apprehend anyone who does not behave according to prescribed codes. They arrive within seconds if someone mistakenly sits on the grass to look at the lake.

Milano Due, entirely managed by a single private interest, represents a clear alternative to the city. It is clean, orderly, and safe, easy to get to by car, well served for sports, and graced with a nicely groomed landscape. There are no class differences here, because the housing costs and maintenance fees require an upper-middle-class income. There are none of the traffic jams of the city, nor any of the conflicts among citizens.

Considering the political success of Milano Due's developer, the founder of Forza Italia ("Go Italy," meant to sound like a soccer cheer)—the most significant new political party since the restructurings of 1989—one has to consider the project as an ideological narrative: it is a well-controlled place without civic participation, the social premises of which are grounded in sport and consumer activity.

The center of Dallas has, during the past thirty years, become a phantom city, with monumental skyscrapers, vast parking lots, a minimum of productive activity during the work day, and an eerie emptiness after sunset. Milan will never be afflicted with such a feeling of civic abandon, but the increasing flight of the middle classes toward its edges for dwelling and shopping is gradually creating a political and economic vacuum. As the center city loses importance, no longer reproducing the needs of daily life, it becomes increasingly rhetorical as the icon of a public realm that no longer requires civic participation. The form of the city, emptied of civic productivity and purpose, tends to crystallize into a museum of the past, a place where citizens are at best a distant memory.

How to Guide Tourism Toward Civic Life

It is the responsibility of municipal authorities to give direction to tourism before it completely uproots the life of cities, and it is a job that requires the same comprehensiveness and urgency as preparations against terrorism. Behind the postcard city is evidence of social and environmental decay, which will continue to increase if policy decisions continue to be formulated according to tourist criteria. To abandon the city to simulation endangers urban life as much as terrorist threats. Tourism and terrorism are not interdependent but simultaneous phenomena that require a clear strategic response. It is only through the maintenance of productive functions in a city that citizens can feel their participation as the makers of their environment and offer resistance to the postcard city. And it is only a city that encourages a twenty-four-hour-a-day mixture of programs that can feel more accountable and secure from crime and terror. Participation is the essential factor in both liveliness and vigilance. As was illustrated in the frescoes of Ambrogio Lorenzetti on the walls of Siena's city hall more than six hundred years ago, the basis of human freedom is justice, which can only be achieved through civic participation. I propose the following correctives for guiding tourism toward the defense of civic life.

Redistribute the Gaze

Too much attention is given to the monumental core of cities and to artifacts that are prized as historically authentic. The interests of tourism need to be integrated with real life and in a variety of urban spaces. Instead of focusing touristic consumption in the center, the cultural planners of municipalities should consider inverse movements that shift the attention away from the center; it would be more interesting to put social housing and new productive spaces in historic buildings, as is currently being done in Barcelona's 22@district, while moving new cultural institutions to the edge, as Barcelona has also done with its Forum 2004 district, a culture park located seven miles from the center. Paris, which has no shortage of new or revitalized attractions at its center, in the 1990s developed a series of new parks on its edges: La Villette, Parc Citroen, and Parc Bercy, which have become new poles of culture and leisure, greatly relieving some of the pressure at the center. A city like Florence, which is suffocating because of an excess of tourists at its center, in the moment that it decided to double the capacity of the Uffizi museum could have made a radical choice to move the Botticellis to the suburbs and diffuse the cultural attractions of the center. Two works by Renzo Piano offer good examples of how to reorient the gaze of tourism: in Amsterdam, his ship-shaped science museum, the New Metropolis, or NEMO, finished in 1996; and, in Rome, the beetle-like music halls of Parco della Musica, opened in 2001. They both create a monumental presence of uncanny forms on the city's edge and provide a rich cultural program that has become a civic as well as tourist attraction. In Amsterdam, the copper-covered prow of NEMO is perilously poised above the highway that plunges under the Ij canal, leading away from the historic center. Two unanticipated public spaces developed through the intervention: a ramp leading to the building's amphitheater-like roof and an interior piazza with cafés, paved the brick of the historic city. One can visit the museum, modeled loosely on the program of San Francisco's Exploratorium, or simply hang out in the public spaces, getting good views of the city. In Rome, the three concert halls, covered with lead shields, are grouped like three colossal scarabs, overlooking an outdoor amphitheater in the Olympic Flaminia district, about three miles from the city gates of the Porta del Popolo. A hanging garden has been raised around the complex to insulate it from the traffic noises and smells of a very busy elevated artery. The variety of cultural functions gathered around its central amphitheater piazza—three museums (one devoted to the Roman villa found during the excavations for the foundations), a bookshop, café, and concert halls, plus a vast garden space—have made it a destination for a variety of planned and improvised activities, not unlike the feeling of St. Peter's Square.

Parco della Musica by Renzo Piano, Rome, 2000.

Democratic Attractions

When programming new cultural facilities, administrations should not overlook the human resources of disadvantaged or marginalized communities. Public parks are for everyone; museums, however, are usually for an economic elite. An interesting corrective to the typically ethnocentric conception of the city as consumer good occurred in Houston at the Project Row Houses. Organized in the early 1990s by African-American artist, Rick Lowe, in a black neighborhood that was in serious decline, a series of twenty-two shotgun houses, which were built in the 1930s as rental units, were renovated for cultural and social uses. Eight of the houses serve as gallery space for changing installations, two are used for community educational programs, and another ten serve a program of transitional housing and guidance to single mothers. The artists, sponsored by local art museums, are invited to make exhibitions that last five months; the young mothers can stay for as long as two years. In the mean time, Project Row Houses has attracted both a wide audience of art enthusiasts and the local support of neighborhood gardeners. Whites and blacks, rich and poor, come for different purposes and become aware of each other in an inspired setting.

The everyday crosses into tourism. Project Row Houses, Houston, Texas, 1990s.

Making Those Who Profit More Responsible

With the onslaught of globalism, cities have come into competition as the settings for commerce and tourism. Each one attempts to organize the biggest convention centers, sports facilities, trade fairs, and amusement attractions to garner the most income from visitors. Behind all the movement of people and consumer activity are immense multinational interests, which often reap great profits from the publicly funded services that are available as part of any city's infrastructure: water, sewerage, transportation, and, above all, roads. Often those who stand to gain the most from the urban situation are the least responsible for its maintenance. It is thus a political question to restructure the exploitation and payment for resources. San Francisco has for two decades imposed a hotel tax to try to compensate for the visitors' burden on local services, but this only throws the responsibility on individual tourists. Recently such Italian tourist cities as Florence and Siena have required every tour bus to pay a fee toward the maintenance of the streets; but, again, it is a cost that is deferred onto the individual consumer and not absorbed by multinational profit makers. One must ask in all situations how a more equitable balance can be established between public expenses and private profits.

Incentives for Production

The most devastating effect of tourism is the parasitical relationship it has with local economies, discouraging their productive base in favor of tourist services. It would be much easier to protect a place's cultural autonomy if out of every expense that goes toward marketing the tourist environment a portion is redirected to sustaining the productive base. Although it has not been scrupulously applied, Italy's 1985 law for *agriturismo*, which sponsored tourist facilities on working farms, is nonetheless a good place to begin a theory of how to maintain production. In Tuscany and a few other regions of Italy, the law required that if a working farm were equipped for tourism, it should only take thirty percent of its income from hospitality, leaving the rest to be generated from agriculture. In this way, it was hoped, the economy of farmers would be assisted without jeopardizing the agricultural landscape and its productive base. Unfortunately, the proceeds from tourism are much greater than those of agriculture, and tourism has frequently become the sole function of country sites. Many farms have been completely redesigned with incongruous swimming pools and tennis courts (the same features that sell Milano Due and Las Colinas), which have little to do with the traditions of the local landscape. Still, the Tuscan countryside has been helped by the original law to maintain its integrity, while regions where the law was not applied, such as Lombardy and the Veneto, are noticeably less protected. To think of a place of tourism as a place of production that needs incentives could greatly help maintain a more varied social fabric.

Integration with Daily Life

The hermetically enclosed places for the citizen-tourist have been organized for the goals of consumerism. If the experiences of a place could be complicated with the diverse needs of daily life, then the presence of the citizen-tourist would assume its proper dimension as a subcategory of social life. In Lucerne, a Swiss city with a long tradition of tourism, a recent intervention by Jean Nouvel shows how to combine daily life with tourism. Next to the Santiago Calatrava–designed train station (1984), and touching the shore of Lake Lucerne, a concert hall/convention center (2000) is covered with dark-green evanescent panels. The visor-like roof juts out as an immense horizontal plane. Inside, one finds a connection to the station, a new bus depot, a small art gallery, a café and restaurant, a multilevel garage, a grand outdoor deck, and a piazza-like foyer into which a small channel of water from the lake has been allowed to permeate. The cultural program and flux of tourists have been integrated with the daily life of the station. Tourists come for the natural features of the lake and mountains, citizens come for the concerts and transportation, and the vitality of the place thrives on the encounter of the two. It is an excellent example of how to avoid the discrimination of one sector in favor of another, of the sort of mixed program that should be every city's dream for civic revival.

Tourist functions well integrated with citizens' needs. Concert Hall/Convention Center by Jean Nouvel, Lucerne, 1998.

3

Jump-cut Urbanism

Cinema, the Automobile, and the
New Code of Urban Perception

Speed and fragmentation. Offramps of La Défense, Paris.

When the Pedestrian Becomes a Driver

How is it possible that people allowed themselves to live in a world without pedestrian streets? For centuries, the street, protected by the continuous walls of urban blocks, was the semantic foundation of urban life, around which the meaning of the everyday was woven. Michel de Certeau explained the essence of the pedestrian street:

> The ordinary practitioners of the city...make use of spaces that cannot be seen; their knowledge of them is as blind as that of lovers in each other's arms. The paths that correspond in this intertwining, unrecognized poem in which each body is an element signed by many others, elude legibility. It is as though the practices organizing a bustling city were characterized by their blindness (de Certeau 1990).

During the twentieth century the urban dweller became increasingly dependent on the automobile and gradually lost the "blindness" of the lover's embrace, learning to live without the corridor streets of the traditional city. Sprawl relates to a different sense of scale and to the speed of cars and is bereft of intimacy. Urban space, which was previously contained, is now without limits. The rhythm of daily life, which before the automobile was defined by the movements of one's body, is now determined by the mechanical devices in the city. The automobile has upset the balance of time and space in the pedestrian-scaled environment.

One of the choicest icons for representing the intimacy of the pre-industrial street is Sebastiano Serlio's *Tragic Scene* (1542), a depiction of a Renaissance stage set that communicates the unity of space

Automobiles interrupt the perspective street. Serlio's *Tragic Scene*.

and time in the continuous prospects of perspective facades leading to a vanishing point beyond the city gate. All of the elements relate harmoniously to the proportions of the human body. For centuries in the West, the perspectival scene accurately described the city street as the theater of daily life.

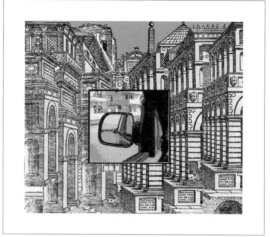

What happens to Serlio's scene when it is invaded by automobiles? The basic dimensions change and upset the proportions of the surroundings. On one hand, cars do not adapt easily to pedestrian-scaled environments, and, on the other, a city made of alleys and piazzas rejects

The rearview mirror fragments space and time like cinematic montage.

these outsize intruders. Serlio's *Tragic Scene* is too confined and cannot easily be equipped for parking or fast-moving traffic. The dimensions of a car (ten feet by six feet) are not compatible with historic streets, which are often only six feet wide. Parked cars become annoying obstacles, while moving cars create spatial fragmentation. The driver, in the attempt to negotiate vehicular movement or in the search for a parking space, sees the street in a different, furtive way. The perspective guidelines dissolve with changes in speed; the car moves at least ten times faster than the pedestrian, and thus the vanishing points seen through a speeding windshield become kaleidoscopic. For a driver, buildings, signs, and background perspectives are arranged much like a sequence of shots assembled for a film, and when the driver uses the rearview mirror, the extraordinary phenomenon of seeing forward and backward simultaneously occurs just like the montage of a cinematic jump cut. Instead of being focused on a single vanishing point, the perspectives have been multiplied and the only fixed point left is the driver.

With the advent of the automobile, the theatrical order of the urban street was converted into a cinematic one, composed of long shots, closeups, pans, tracking shots, and, above all, the accelerated montage of jump cuts. To propose a jump cut urbanism does not mean that a clear method of design based on the cinematic metaphor will necessarily emerge, as much as it attempts to reason about change in the dominant modes of perception. While one is driving, images of the city race by one's windshield in a series of fragments that are received at various speeds. This new perception is closer to cinema than to the fixed proscenium of the theater. Cinema and the automobile, two myth-producing products of industrial culture, reached a convergence of popular consumption in the 1920s, first in the U.S. and then elsewhere. From the moment that their impact altered the cognition of urban space, the form of the city would no longer be the same.

Many of the morphological changes to the city were determined by the new spatial requirements of the automobile. Almost immediately the dense

An abandoned drive-in movie theater.

urban fabric of the center was eroded to serve automobiles: urban corners were sacrificed to gas stations and drive-ins, city blocks were leveled for parking lots, and entire districts were demolished to create off-ramps for the interstate highway network. Highways, ring roads, feeder roads, and flyovers became the basis of a new city scale, attracting settlement away from the center and fragmenting what was left of its fabric with interventions that facilitated automobile access. American cities changed quickly into polycentric territories of scattered development. In such cities as Atlanta, Houston, Detroit, and Los Angeles, as much as seventy-five to eighty percent of urban land is paved, either for circulation or parking. Sprawl began along the high-speed lanes in a landscape punctuated by isolated buildings and composed of ambiguous in-between spaces. In the mean time, human consciousness became accustomed to the magic of cinematic montage, familiar with its fragmentation of time and space. The filmic jump cut tore to pieces Serlio's perspectival scene, opening the way for cars to drive through it.

The Unstoppable Rise of Ford

At the beginning of the twentieth century, mostly because of the personal success of Henry Ford, the automobile was transformed from a luxury item into an indispensable tool for everyday life. It is difficult to discern whether the changes made to urban space were completely the fault of automobiles, but the cars definitely carried an imperative for the use of urban space. It was a tool with highly destructive potential, but even more destructive were the public administrations, stunned and seduced by the power of automobiles. The problems of traffic and parking exerted a mythic pressure on cities that at times seemed more violent than they were in actuality.

In the same years that Ford revolutionized automobile production, the U.S. experienced a synthesis of political and industrial power. As revealed in 1930 by Paul Hoffman, the vice president of Studebaker Motors, "The automobile industry is intensely interested in the progress of city planning—for the very sound reason that a continual increase in motor sales in the U.S.A. depends largely on developing more efficient traffic accommodation in metropolitan areas" (Foster 1991). The combined power of the motor and petrol industries during the 1950s, when one job in six was related to them, was fundamental to the redesign of urban centers. Charles E. Wilson, ex-CEO of General Motors, made a rather bold statement on being inducted as Dwight D. Eisenhower's Secretary of Defense: "What's good for General Motors is good for the country." It's a statement that underlines the ascendancy of the military-industrial complex that has to this day dominated the political system. In the current administration of George W. Bush, the majority of the key players have been executives or on the board of directors for major petrol interests.

The impact of the automobile on urban design has been as strong as its psychological effects. Perhaps only the advent of monotheism has had as great a psycho-social impact on urban culture. As Roland Barthes explains, in *Mythologies* (1957): "I think that the automobile today is the near equivalent of the great gothic cathedrals: by this I mean the creations of an age, passionately conceived by anonymous craftsmen, consumed in image if not in use, by an entire people who aspire to it as a perfectly magic object." Lewis Mumford, the great American critic, made a similar, if more bitter, cosmological claim: "For the current American way of life is founded not just on motor transportation but on the religion of the motorcar, and the sacrifices that people are prepared to make for this religion stand outside the realm of rational criticism" (Mumford 1963).

Henry Ford was the undisputed prophet in this act of mass conversion. In 1903, he founded the Ford Motor Company as one of more than a hundred automobile makers. Ten years later, he controlled forty-five percent of the market, and by the beginning of the 1920s he had gained a nearly complete monopoly. His entrepreneurial success was due not only to technological innovations in mass production but also to remarkable concessions to factory workers. In 1912, Ford introduced the assembly-line system, which allowed twenty-nine workers to assemble a motor in only ninety-three minutes. This lowered the cost of production of the Model T from $825 in 1910 to $345 in 1916, reaching its all-time low of $290 in 1927. This incredible drop in price destroyed his competitors. Then, at the same time that Ford cornered the market, he decided to double workers' salaries and impose a fixed eight-hour day, turning producers into consumers. While the assembly line greatly dehumanized the work process, the advantages in terms of salaries and hours were concrete gains for labor.

With his industrial pragmatism, Ford brought the car to the people and gave birth to the age of motorization. He was seriously considered as a candidate for the presidential election of 1923 despite his earlier failed campaign for governor of Michigan. Fordism, the efficient exploitation of the division of mechanized labor, was seen as a new method of production to be applied to all levels of society. Ford's autobiography, published in 1925, was the international bestseller of its time, studied assiduously by those interested in power: the Soviets, Hitler, and in architectural circles Le Corbusier. During the same years, Ford furnished 25,000 tractors to the USSR before helping to set up factories there based on his model (Cohen 1995). The Volkswagen, sponsored by Hitler in 1935, was directly inspired by the story of the Model T, as was Le Corbusier's proposal for the *voiture maximum* in 1928, which anticipated the *deux chevaux* later produced by Citröen.

Fordism not only changed the methods of mass production but also initiated the fulfillment of a shorter work week, more leisure time, and more democratic access to the automobile. Almost without notice, the urban parameters of American cities radically changed. It was no accident that sprawl began in the U.S. In a young country with relatively new and rootless cities, there was less resistance, physically or socially, to modernization. And, due to nineteenth-century fire codes, the streets of American cities, typically sixty to one hundred feet wide, were already twice as wide as those of Europe and thus ready for heavy vehicular traffic. The power of Detroit was instrumental in instigating sprawl, but one should never underestimate the role of consumers in changing the environment. Already in the late 1920s, one in five Americans owned a car, and eighty percent of the cars produced in the world were concentrated in the U.S. Other industrialized nations, like England and France, had about one car per forty people.

Another factor to consider in the rise of automobiles is the fusion of utility with eros. The car was not just a practical means of individual transportation but a veritable chariot of love. In a system of consumer desires, it promised freedom of individual movement, the thrill of speed, the flight from the city, amorous encounters at motels, and the site for the first romantic experiences for teenagers. As an instrument of desire, the automobile surpassed rationality and took advantage of the urban system.

Toward the end of the Depression in the 1930s, another idea was generated around the sale of automobiles: marketing. Motor companies used advertising, styling, and novel colors to simulate the interests of the ideal consumer, the one whose personal identity would be reinforced through the act of acquisition. In this way, the car became the fundamental article of the consumer society, the first act (and shopping cart) for a succession of acquisitions. The psychological bond between consumer and the automobile goes even deeper since in the U.S. the principal identity card is the driver's license.

Il faut tuer la rue corridor (Death to the Street)

A century before Ford's triumph, the locomotive initiated a series of stresses on the urban fabric of great cities. London, Berlin, Paris, and New York underwent traumatic interventions to accommodate train lines, often witnessing brutal demolitions and drastic separations of one part of town from another. In all of the little towns along Italy's Via Emilia, for example, from Piacenza to Rimini, the railroad neatly separated urban from industrial quarters. The great difference in the transformations carried out for the automobile, of course, was that rails are fixed. They don't take over public space, and they leave their travelers at determined locations.

The speed of the trains unquestionably affected the awareness of space-time, anticipating the new perception from the automobile; from the train window, however, one looked laterally at panoramas flashing by, a bit like the tracking shot in cinema. This kind of shot is in fact obtained from a moving camera that has been mounted on rails, thus sharing the same technology. In contrast to the view from the car, the view from the train rarely is able to fragment urban space; the rail passenger was removed physically from urban space, often hoisted above or thrust below grade, and set on a fixed itinerary that ended in the public space of a station, where the rider resumed a pedestrian existence, in a taxi, tram, or bus. The train passenger was necessarily passive; the driver of a car is active, deciding the itinerary, when to change direction, how to change gears, or when to stop, or get out. The driver thus behaves more like the film director, assembling bits of disconnected shots.

The first urban master plans were a response to rapid demographic growth, industrial production, and mechanical means of transportation. The Paris of Napoleon III and Baron Haussmann (1853–71) provides the most dramatic example: the great city of two million inhabitants was rethought in terms of *reseaux* "networks" for services, including aqueducts, markets, sewers, parks, and a hundred miles of new boulevards (sixty to one hundred feet wide—at 360 feet, the widest is Avenue Foch). During the violent transformation of Paris, which necessitated massive demolitions, the city was compensated with the planting of four hundred thousand mature street trees, supplying a green armature for the boulevards. The great width of Parisian boulevards was often much wider than the six-story facades that lined them were tall. The exceptional emptiness of boulevard Richard Lenoir, for example, still seems uncanny, and the paintings of Gustave Caillebotte convey the disturbing dimensions of the reconstructed industrial city. Aside from the hygienic, aesthetic, and circulatory motives behind Haussmann's renewals, the most sincere motivation was in the name of military defense against popular uprisings.

The first real attempt to deal with the automobile as a factor in urban planning came with the next generation of planners in Paris. The city architect Eugène Hénard published his thesis on modernizing Paris in 1907 with several lasting innovations, including the ubiquitous *rond point*, or traffic circle. The idea of inducing a one-way circulation in a round figure was first established under Hénard's direction at the Arc de Triomphe. A concept that would be more influential during the second half of the twentieth century was to conceive of the city in terms of layers, isolating pedestrians on a different level from vehicles. Despite the pragmatic approach of French planners, the nineteenth century Parisian street never lost its connection to the perspectival codes of the Renaissance, and remained a void in a compact fabric of solids.

No one seemed able to predict the impact of automobiles on the city at the beginning of the twentieth century. The first presentiment that machines were about to take over the environment appeared in the various manifestoes of the Futurists between 1907 and 1914. The young architect Antonio Sant'Elia wrote in *L'Architettura futurista*: "We must invent and rebuild the Futurist city as if it were an immense factory yard, tumultuous,

Baron Haussmann's jump in scale with forty-meter wide boulevards, Paris, 1850s.

flexible, mobile, dynamic in all of its parts; and the modern house like a gigantic machine" (Sant'Elia 1914). The Futurists exalted speed and movement, favoring the destruction of the old and the impetuous new. They imagined an ephemeral city that would constantly rebuild itself. Perhaps the only true realization of the Futurist ideal of integrating machines with architecture was the Fiat automobile factory, Il Lingotto, built for the Fiat company in Turin by Giacomo Matté Trucco (1916–22). The Lingotto factory was the true precursor of a jump cut method because it willingly integrated the movement of automobiles into its structure: the automobile moved up from floor to floor until it emerged as a finished product on the roof, where the test track demonstrated a synthesis of speed and architecture.

Close to the avant-garde imperatives of Futurism, Le Corbusier, in the 1920s, designed a terrifying vision of a new metropolis suited to the scale of automobiles. After receiving a car as a gift from his client Raoul La Roche, the architect learned for himself the difficulties of driving in the narrow spaces of the historic city. His Contemporary City for Three Million (1922) was an extreme proposal based on the efficient movement of machines and democratic access to green spaces. While proposing for the center an improbable airport on a layered quatrefoil-shaped platform, under which were a train station, a bus depot, and the highway interchange, he insisted that, through vertical expansion, the city could have both a higher density of population and a greater amount of open green space. Le Corbusier's central freeway appears to be twelve lanes wide (about the width of avenue Foch), and the business skyscrapers of the center were forty stories; neither of these types had yet to be built in Europe. The human scale was completely absent in the Contemporary City, and pedestrian life was confined to vast gardens, segregated from the roads since there were no streets or plazas. In a later article, Le Corbusier would proclaim, *"Il faut tuer la rue corridor,"* or "Death to the street." In his proposals for cities without pedestrian streets he inverted the relation of figure-ground with isolated figures surrounded by green voids. This model of the tower in the park anticipates many of the incongruous spatial relationships of sprawl.

One of the most memorable pages of Le Corbusier's 1925 treatise *Towards a New Architecture*, juxtaposes images of two Doric temples, shown in a sequence of stylistic progression, and of two automobiles, treated the same way. This parallel implied that architecture and machines could and should be judged by the same criteria. In the final pages of the book, he published the Lingotto factory, the happy union of architecture and automobile, as a form of conclusion. In later publications, the photographs of his 1920s Purist villas always included an automobile in the foreground as an element of scale. For his most famous work, the Villa Savoye at Poissy, the curve of the ground-floor plan was determined by the turning radius of a car as it moved to the garage.

In 1925, Le Corbusier acquired a new car, a Voisin, probably under the aegis of his new client, Gabriel Voisin. Voisin, who produced automobiles and airplanes and even attempted to mass-produce houses, was seduced by Le Corbusier into becoming the sponsor of his 1925 Plan Voisin for Paris. This offered the first modern lesson of tabula rasa planning, for which Le Corbusier far exceeded Haussmann's penchant for demolitions, proposing to knock down the entire quarter of the Marais and replace it with an elevated highway, forty-story skyscrapers, and vast gardens. Despite his personal lack of success in the replanning of Paris, Le Corbusier's method legitimated innumerable tabula rasa projects in Paris and elsewhere.

In his treatise, *La Ville Radieuse* (1935), Le Corbusier added to his repertoire of urban designs a revealing diagram known as "the modern situation," which explains how the relationship of services to modern life favors the solution of the tower in the park. A large eye, representing a dweller in a high-rise apartment, is shown in a unit with a double-height section, an elevator connects the apartment to the ground, and four lines lead from the base to electricity, gas, telephone, and water. Spreading beneath the tower is grass and trees. Le Corbusier's disconnected eye, suspended above the world, was meant to convey the notion of individual liberty made possible by technology. Inadvertently, the drawing foretold the anomie that such isolated environments would breed in suburban situations and the profound solitude created by the distancing devices of modern life.

Kinopravda, or I Am a Camera

The cyclopic eye drawn by Le Corbusier, surveying the sprawl of the future, is contemporary with another gigantic eye: the kino-eye of Dziga Vertov, icon of revolutionary Soviet cinema. Dziga Vertov was the pseudonym of Dennis Kaufman, a young filmmaker from the Ukraine who entered the avant-garde circles of Bolshevik Russia in the 1920s. Inspired by the theories of constructivism in the visual arts and the theories of montage of Kuleshov, he wrote numerous manifestoes for a constructivist and revolutionary cinema.

> I am kino-eye. I am a mechanical eye. I, a machine, show you the world as only I can see it.
>
> Now and forever I free myself from human immobility, I am in constant motion, I draw near, then away from objects, I crawl under, I climb onto them. I move apace with the muzzle of a galloping horse, I plunge full speed into a crowd, I outstrip running soldiers, I fall on my back, I ascend with an airplane, I plunge and soar together with plunging and soaring bodies. Now I, a camera, fling myself along their resultant, maneuvering in the chaos of movement, recording movement, starting with movements composed of the most complex combinations. Freed from the rule of sixteen to seventeen frames per second, free of the limits of time and space, I put together any given points in the universe, no matter where I've recorded them. My path leads to the creation of a fresh perception of the world. I decipher in a new way a world unknown to you. (1923)

In his treatise/film, *Man with a Movie Camera* (1929), a work that had little distribution until it was rediscovered in 1970, Vertov narrates a day in the life of a city. In the film, he reveals all of the means of its making, showing in closeup the union of his eye and the viewfinder of the camera, the cameraman hovering above the city, scissors cutting the film, and the film editor assembling pieces of film. In certain scenes, he uses split-screen techniques to show the fragmentation caused by machines moving through the city. The jump cut, the transition from shot to shot, is for Vertov the essence of modern cognition, a means of obtaining the truth, or what he calls *kinopravda*.

The year before Vertov's film was finished, Buster Keaton released a commercially successful comedy *The Cameraman* (1928). Without any avant-garde or revolutionary pretensions, Keaton employed many of the same techniques of the Russian theorist. In the story, an inept cameraman creates amusing accidents of montage, such as the improbable appearance of a battleship on Fifth Avenue. He also plays with the idea of cinema as truth when, in order to obtain a news scoop, he instigates a riot in Chinatown that he can then film as news. The same devices that Vertov championed as vehicles of kinopravda become in Keaton's viewfinder elements of slapstick and ridicule. Both filmmakers—one with gags, the other with poetry—investigated the power of the cinematic language of montage. Cinema's capacity to recompose time and space changed the way people understood the city. The jump cut, the violent fragmentation of montage, would become a normal part of human cognition, a code of perception that would surpass the norms of the perspectival code that preceded it.

Futurama: The Will to Motorization

The birth of jump cut urbanism accompanied the emergence of modern freeways and flyovers. The first of these was the forty-mile stretch known as Milano-Laghi, built in 1924. It was followed by numerous other private initiatives that were eventually consolidated in 1938 by the Fascist state planning agency and programmed as a three thousand mile network, the progress of which was interrupted by World War II. Nazi Germany, with the slogan "the will to motorization," had a similar goal of three thousand miles of autobahn and by 1939 had already realized two thousand miles of it, attracting the admiration of the American auto industry, including the executives of General Motors. Planned by Fritz Todt and the landscape designer Alwin Seifert, who geared the new roads to ecological and picturesque principles, the autobahn was a favorite subject of Nazi propaganda films and probably the most explicit product of "reactionary modernism," the combination of high engineering and military utilitarianism blended with the mythic values of land.

Aside from isolated experiences, such as the 1924 "superhighway" in Detroit and the first flyovers introduced in the 1920s intersection-free parkways connecting to Manhattan, the divided highway would be introduced in the U.S. during the 1930s. The vast American highway system became the subject of large publicworks campaigns during the Depression. In 1932, four percent of the unemployed were put to work building highways. The best of these interventions was the fifty-kilometer Merrit Parkway between New Haven and Manhattan, with coordinated landscapes by Gilmore D. Clarke; it was completed in 1938.

The most important act of promotion for a national highway system—and by extension for the legitimation of sprawl—came with the Futurama pavilion of the 1939 World Fair in New York City. There the automobile and cinema joined in a perfect union to celebrate the imperative of fast roads. Sponsored by General Motors, which had surpassed Ford in the 1930s as the largest motor company, the exhibitions and styling were handled by Norman Bel Geddes, who had published a book promoting highways. The exterior of the pavilion was the first true work of architectural expressionism in the U.S.; a colossal, monolithic curve, it was an icon of the aerodynamic, teardrop aesthetic applied to car bodies. The multimedia contents inside were organized like a film. The spectator was seated on a conveyor belt (a technique borrowed from the assembly line) and given a fifteen-minute ride through models at different scales, clips of the city of the future, and the city of 1960. This view of animated models, staffed with fifty thousand tiny moving vehicles, was seen first at a scale of 1:10,000, then of 1:200, then of 1:25, leading to the final jump cut: upon exiting, the spectator walked into a full-scale version of an elevated pedestrian crosswalk of the city of 1960, and looked down on current GM cars, anachronistically displayed in a traffic jam on the street below. Futurama's city of the future looked similar to what Dallas or Phoenix have become today, with scattered nuclei of high-rises and lots of elevated freeways. One of the models proposed an eighteen-lane freeway with the same mandate as Le Corbusier: to separate the pedestrian from the automobile.

The link between the sponsor and the promotion of a national highway system was transparent. The motor company understood that it was in its own interest to lobby for automobile infrastructure, and it would shortly mobilize against public-rail transportation. In addition to the five million visitors to the Futurama pavilion, at least twenty million people saw the ten-minute film "New Horizons" which was based on its contents. More than those of Le Corbusier, Frank Lloyd Wright, or any other major architect, this single exhibition created the cultural acceptance of sprawl. Through jump-cut techniques, it sold the message of freeways, urban-renewal demolitions, and a city built at the scale of the automobile.

After World War II, the U.S. produced legislation for the largest freeway system in the world. Approved as the Interstate Highway Act in 1956, it initially projected a network of thirty-seven thousand miles of interurban highway, of which seven thousand would be within city limits. The demolitions recommended for the urban freeways, which were linked to those of the "urban renewal" programs of the 1949 Housing Act, led to the heaviest nonmilitary destruction of cities ever executed. The centers of Philadelphia, San Francisco, St.

Louis, Newark, Boston, and other large cities were devastated in the name of rebuilding neighborhoods and inserting highway structures. Every mile of freeway required forty acres of land. The demolitions in Boston were the most tragic from a historical point of view, eliminating the dense fabric of the only "medieval" city in the U.S. To build the central artery, an elevated freeway that crossed the center city, more than twenty thousand residents were evicted, and in the 1960s another thirty thousand were eliminated from the West End, most of them African-American. In this way, central Boston was turned into a tabula rasa without the help of aerial bombardment. It is thus a supreme irony that twenty-five years after the destruction of Scollay Square, Boston voters approved a referendum for the removal of the elevated freeway, forcing an underground solution and necessitating one of the most ambitious infrastructural projects of all time, the so-called Big Dig (1995–2005).

The compelling success of Futurama prepared the way for jump cut urbanism to take hold of the imagination. This promotion of the "will to motorization" helped replace the theatrical perception of the street with a code of urban perception based on the scale of the automobile and the fragmented vision it generated. It provoked a crisis of meaning in the collective spaces of center cities, some of which were extinguished forever by implementation of tabula rasa.

Forty acres of land for every mile of freeway fragments the city. MacArthur Freeway under construction, Oakland, California, 1960s.

"Montage Is Therefore Conflict"

The disorderliness of many contemporary edge settlements seems like a series of pictures put together by random accident, without a narrative structure. What is missing in sprawl, even in the most planned parts of it, is a sense of coordinated montage. As with any art form, film montage needs to contend with theory; otherwise it will remain without direction. According to the great Russian director Sergei Eisenstein, montage should be approached as a matter of conflict. In one of his theoretical texts, he queried the effects of the jump cut:

Is this not exactly what we do as film makers...when we create the monstrous disproportion among the parts of a normal fact, dismembering it suddenly with a close up of hands that touch, a middle shot of a struggle, and a detail of opened eyes, thus disintegrating the fact through montage on different levels? Or when we show an enlarged eye, twice the size of a man?! Mixing these monstrous incongruities, we recompose a disintegrated fact into a unity according to our own vision: according to how we interpret this fact. ("The cinematographic principle and the ideogram," 1929)

Among the cinematic elements that Eisenstein chose to contrast, many seem to possess architectural character: he speaks of planes, volumes, masses, and depth.

The famous Odessa Steps sequence of Eisenstein's *Battleship Potemkin* (1925) can be read as a project for jump cut urbanism. The narrative is arranged around a series of contrasts between shifting points of view, close ups and long shots, darkness and light, juxtaposed camera angles, details and panoramas. The audience follows a succession of contrasts: the soldiers with their rifles leveled, the people fleeing down the stairs, a mother with her wounded child in her arms climbing the steps to challenge them, the shadows of the rifles closing in on her, a closeup to her face while in the background the troops are more regular and geometrically organized, and finally the intersection of the soldiers' shadows and her body, culminating in her execution.

If jump cut urbanism were a real method of architectural design, applied according to the cinematic criteria of Eisenstein, then it would follow a structural narrative that is capable of coordinating the "monstrous incongruities" of conflicting architectural fragments and awkward voids. An urbanist director would elucidate the components that make up a city, each with its own scale and time, trying to tie them together in a common plan. According to Eisenstein's observation, "montage is therefore conflict," a true jump cut urbanism would reflect the rhythm of perceptual contrasts: mixing together speed with repose, creating the possibility of movement and access, facilitating different points of view. It would allow enough distance and yet cultivate intimacy, so that one could comfortably go by foot or by car.

The Plinth and the Highway

After World War II, a few projects seem particularly consistent with the notion of jump cut urbanism. The most important is without doubt the U.N. Building in New York (1947–52). Directly influenced by Le Corbusier and built to the designs of Oscar Niemeyer under the guidance of Wallace K. Harrison, the U.N. campus occupies a six-block site that is treated as a plinth set off from the Manhattan grid. A large hanging garden cantilevers over the fast traffic of FDR Drive to give a panoramic view of the East River. The figure of the oblong glass tower comes in and out of view as one drives under the plinth or skirts it along a submerged section of First Avenue on the other side. The complex mixes the dynamism of the fast flanking roads with the slowness of the lateral streets, intentionally contrasting car movement with pedestrian pace.

Another case of a willful conflict of vehicles and pedestrians was designed at the same time for the center of Caracas, the Centro Bolívar by Cipriano Domínguez. The two twenty-five-story office towers enclose a plinth that is used as a public gathering space. The eight-lane Avenida Bolívar plunges under the plinth, while transverse streets penetrate at grade level for the bus stop and pedestrian access. The two underground parking levels have open views to the plinth. The two speeds of automobiles and pedestrians have been gracefully intertwined to create a sort of teeter-totter of nearness and distance—similar to the cinematic jump cut.

A montage in an oil boomtown. Centro Bolívar by Cipriano Domínguez, Caracas, 1952.

During the boom years of the 1950s in Caracas, due to its new petrol riches, the Venezuelan state planned one of the most ambitious urban-freeway systems in the world; elevated interchanges acquired mythic names such as the "Spider" or the "Crab." The enthusiasm for automobile acces-

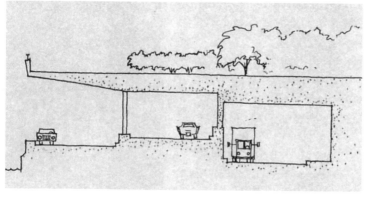

Manhattan jump-cut. United Nations Building, New York City, 1949–52.

sibility led to an extraordinary plan for a shopping center that would integrate vehicular movement, parking, and a continuous band of shops along an ascending spiral road. El Helicoide (1956–57), designed by Jorge Romero, coils around a hill and culminates in a polyhedron dome. It was never finished, due to the sudden defect of the military government with which the developers were in close collaboration, and it has thus remained an aborted monument to the jump cut ideal: a building that allowed a coordinated narrative of constantly changing perspectives as one drove seven 360-degree turns to the top of the spiral. After twenty years of abandonment, the structure of El Helicoide was eventually expropriated by the state and used as a police station to survey the uncontrollable spread of *ranchos*, spontaneous dwellings that have been built right up to its edges.

When the formal typology of the U.N. complex, a plinth suspended over fast roads and parking, is carried out at a larger scale, it can often cause a disturbing sense of disorientation. Both the Barbican Centre in London and La Défense in Paris, produced during the 1960s, induce a feeling of separation anxiety. The approach in both cases is at an uncomfortable subterranean level, from which one emerges into a beautiful aerial landscape that is completely cut off from the urban system. The feeling of disorientation prevails because it is difficult to perceive the connection back to the ground and the rest of the city. So strong is the sense of entrapment in the Barbican Centre that the management decided to paint a yellow line on the pathways, like the thread of Ariadne, in order to help people find their way out of the enclave.

El Helicoide, by Jorge Romero, Caracas, 1957.

Domesticating the plinth. La Défense, Paris, 1965-2005
(Otto von Sprekelsen is the architect of the arch).

Perhaps the most extensive plinth of all, Louvain la Neuve, a university town in Belgium begun in the 1970s according to a master plan by Victor Gruen, negates the possibilities of cinematic perception, leaving only a sense of being stranded. The entire twenty-block core of the center has been stacked over a two-story parking structure, under which pass the freeway and the interurban train line. The pedestrian network of the upper level imitates the dense fabric of medieval cities, artificially suspended above the infrastructure.

One of the urban projects followed with the most attention during the 1990s was Euralille, a reinterpretation of the jump cut, which proposed a neo-modernist plinth in service as a critical infrastructural node. The master plan, by Rem Koolhaas, aspired to the simultaneity of scales, romanticizing the convergence of high-speed trains, freeways, subways, parking levels, and pedestrian plazas. The intersection of the freeway with the high-speed rail line became the site of the plinth for a multilevel station, metro stop, and parking area. Two office skyscrapers were perched on top of the plinth. Between the old station and the plinth was a wide plaza and a wedge-shaped shopping mall, dotted with three smaller towers for student residences. In the midst of the off-ramps, an egg-shaped convention center completed the program. The architecture of Euralille was treated with less attention to detail than to visual effect, almost as movie sets are: the undulating roofs of Jean Duteuil's station (1995), the boot-shaped tower by Christian de Portzamparc (1995), the scintillating photosensitive skin of Jean Nouvel's shopping mall (1995), the wavy walls of Koolhaas's CongresExpo (1995). Somewhat like the ephemeral modernist city in Jacques Tati's *Playtime* (1967), Euralille's many parts seem ready to disintegrate at any minute—and indeed the leaks are legendary. Despite the technical problems of the buildings—the metro station and the high-speed-rail station frequently flood when it rains—the perceptual goal of jump-cut urbanism has been convincingly achieved, since there is an interlacing of different scales and speeds that permits one to be aware of the montage of space and time. Euralille, with its brash, disposable, and violent interventions, returns to the Futurist project for the city and transmits the same fascination with contrast and juggling of situations that a film like *Pulp Fiction* (1994) does.

Road Movie

Projects like Euralille, which correspond to the criteria of jump cut urbanism, attempt to integrate the speed of vehicles with the design of buildings and public spaces. To conclude this reflection on the impact of automobiles and cinema on spatial perception, I want to consider how pervasive the role of automobiles is in contemporary cinema. From the 1920s onward, the car has been a constant presence in film, a means of allowing the camera to reproduce what it can do best: movement. It is not by chance that the American word for film is movies or that the automobile has always been the privileged agent for making the movies move. From the slapstick scenes of Buster Keaton, who finds himself holding the steering wheel of a car that has collapsed, to the apocalyptic conclusion of Jean Luc Godard's *Weekend* (1967), rife with barbaric accidents and traffic jams, the car is omnipresent as a narrative tool and symbol. It is almost impossible to think of a film set in contemporary times in which the automobile is not present. Even Louis Malle's claustrophobic *My Dinner with André* (1981) ends with a liberating taxi ride. The automobile is in effect the most recognizable context of modern life and the most reliable narrative device.

In Alfred Hitchcock's *Vertigo* (1958), the narrative structure revolves around a car ride through San Francisco that is repeated. The scenes of the city—an apartment on Nob Hill, Coit Tower, Mission Dolores, and the Golden Gate Bridge—are fragments seen by the driver, James Stewart, as he follows the other driver, Kim Novak. The sequence of geographic locations is illogical, but the magic of the jump cuts, which alternate views of the landscape with closeups of the drivers and their cars, gives the impression of coherence. By a strange mechanism, movement becomes the most reliable point of reference.

The importance of automobiles to films has generated a new narrative genre, the road movie, in which characters pass most of the film in the car. *It Happened One Night* (1934), *The Asphalt Jungle* (1950), *Il Sorpasso* (1962), *Psycho* (1960), *Lolita* (1962), *Bonnie and Clyde* (1967), *Easy Rider* (1969), *Badlands* (1973), *Thelma and*

Louise (1991) all belong to this genre. The road movie usually tells of an escape from the city. The car permits the characters to enjoy the liminal status of provisional freedom from the formal or moral constraints of urban situations. Often the story ends with the return to urban order and some sort of sacrifice, either proposing the characters as scapegoats or suggesting that their liminality is a lost ideal. One of the repeated themes in American movies is the idea that individual liberty can be obtained by fleeing in a car. It is almost always stronger than the idea that freedom is the result of the social negotiation of the city.

Film has reinforced the mythic role of the automobile in consumer society. The power of automobiles, despite its deleterious environmental consequences, continues relatively unchallenged. In the U.S., the current number of cars per family is 1.92! And the world is waiting in anxious fear for a billion Chinese to become drivers.

In the 1960s, following the admired example of the three-block Lijnbaan pedestrian shopping street in Rotterdam, many modern urban planners thought it best to create lots of pedestrian streets in order to save the city from automobiles. Quite often, however, the rigid separation of cars and pedestrians led to a sterile and isolated urban situation with awkward empty spaces. Jane Jacobs, the champion of traditional neighborhoods and leader of the struggle against tabula rasa planning and urban freeways, nonetheless recognized the importance of maintaining a certain proximity between automobile and pedestrian spaces. Urban vitality depends on accessibility, and if the pedestrian zones do not intersect with car traffic, they become boring and even dangerous. If parking is too far from one's destination and if the car's path is too far from the urban setting, most shoppers will choose another venue. As Joel Garreau formulated it, "the farthest distance an American will willingly walk before getting into a car: six hundred feet" (Garreau 1991).

Just like cinema, the automobile should be treated by designers of sprawl as a narrative and symbolic device and not simply a utilitarian means of transportation. During the years of urban renewal there was no real need to create the tabula rasa nor to cede the centers of cities to the brutal tyranny of car movement. But today one should not exaggerate in the other direction by excluding the role of the car in the project of the city. The automobile should be used with the same sensibility that a film director uses the rhythm of jump cuts. As in a good movie, the city of jump cut urbanism will integrate different scales, speeds, and points of view into a narrative whole that corresponds to this new code of urban perception.

4

Infrastructure as Art
Toward Urban Ready-mades

La Trinitat, a freeway park by Enric Batlle and Joan Roig, Barcelona, 1992.

The Cathedral of Mobility

Is it permissible while speeding through the complex weave of elevated highway interchanges to succumb to unconditional aesthetic pleasure? To find oneself enchanted by the kinetic flickering of light, thrilled by the power of formidable structural members, intrigued by the vibrant equilibrium between technique and function is indeed a feeling similar to those elicited by works of modern art. Perhaps someday, when traffic is light and seen from a different perspective, these gigantic snarls of concrete and steel will appear to be the cathedrals of the automobile age, sublime works designed by anonymous civil engineers in the name of the principal act of faith of consumer society: mobility. The drive on the spindly aerial ramps entering Naples through the Vomero district is breathtaking, as are sections of the Périfèrique ring road in Paris. The new aerial highways that soar over the commercial districts of Shanghai inspire a reverent awe. And to find oneself in the labyrinthine interchange of Interstate 45 and Highway 59 near downtown Houston is as powerful an experience as coming upon the crossing of Notre Dame de Beauvais.

That said, one cannot deny that highway flyovers are at the same time obvious harbingers of the advancing environmental catastrophe: incorrigible agents of air pollution, noise pollution, traffic accidents, and urban disorientation. Not everyone is willing to recognize them as objects of desire or temples of mass mobility. Works of infrastructure have an underlying utility; they do the dirty work that tends to distance them from the aesthetic realm. Rarely is the beauty of the great viaducts explicitly acknowledged. In truth, the concrete-and-steel ramps incite a painful beauty, either because they connote the grittiness of their function or because they introduce offensive by-products into daily life.

Aside from their functionality as public works, dare one find them beautiful? The aesthetic appreciation of infrastructure belongs to the Romantic criteria of the sublime, best defined by Giovan Battista Piranesi's aphorism "Out of terror pleasure springs" (1767). Piranesi's visions of ancient works of Roman infrastructure, such as the emissarium near Tivoli, juxtapose the human figures as puny

The frightening beauty of a Shanghai elevated exchange.

and insignificant beings against the power of great structures. The sublime's contradictory sentiments of fascination and repulsion became the negative counterpart to Classical taste. Through the essays of Addison and Burke (Copley & Garside 1994) and exposure to Michelangelo and Piranesi, liberal English intellectuals of the eighteenth century embraced the sublime as an important theory and attempted to reproduce the negative experience of it in their picturesque gardens. Fake ruins and highly contrasting topographic elements were intended to capture the "agreeable kind of horror" identified by Addison. Theoretically the sublime opened a discourse on a different type of beauty. Its rhetorical function, in the words of the Romantic poet John Keats, was to exploit "the negative capacity of art."

At the beginning of the twentieth century, avant-garde art movements relied on the critical aspect of the sublime to create an aesthetic discourse. The arguable beauty of dreaded industrial realities became the provocative premise of the first avant-garde manifesto, Filippo Tomaso Marinetti's initiatory "Le Futurisme," published in the leading newspaper of Paris in 1909. Marinetti's delirious eulogy to speed and technique, in which he raves about the beauty of a traffic accident, concludes with the provocation that the "hood ornament of a speeding automobile is more beautiful than the Winged Victory of Samothrace." Marinetti's young protégé, the architect Antonio Sant'Elia, produced a series of views of "la città nuova" in which the working parts of the city—railways, power lines, elevators—were exposed and monumentalized (da Costa Meyer 1995). The Futurist vision was elaborated by Le Corbusier in the 1920s in his terrifying, antisocial urban models, collectively known as *La Ville Radieuse* (1935). Le Corbusier's penchant for the negative can be heard in his gloss on the pragmatic methods of Taylorism as the "horrible but ineluctable future" (von Moos 1979). His vision of a metropolis structured on highways and dotted with isolated high-rises apparently eliminated any reference to public space, which was sacrificed to the priorities of infrastructure.

One of Le Corbusier's more endearing urban projects, in which infrastructure assumes its possibilities as the sublime, is the so-called *Obus* "shrapnel" plan for Algiers, designed during the 1930s. This project for the North African colonial capital proposed an elevated highway, the curves of which followed the lay of the land from the hills to the port. The viaduct led from the European residential districts to the business-center tower, passing over, without disturbing, the dense indigenous district of the Casbah. The supporting concrete frame of the viaduct was to be exploited as an armature into which housing would be inserted, thus obtaining two functions from a single structure. In this hypothesis of how to rebuild Algiers into a modern city, Le Corbusier attempted to apply to public works the same formal criteria he used in his paintings of curvaceous nudes.

As Stanislaus von Moos has noted, Le Corbusier's combination of housing and viaduct was anticipated in his utopian proposal for a linear city built over the rail lines connecting New York to San Francisco (von Moos 1979). Edgar Chambless, a prophet against sprawl, published *Roadtown* in 1910 as the solution to preventing diffused urbanization from destroying America's wilderness and agricultural lands. The roof of his horizontal megastructure was to be developed as hanging gardens and public space. In 1961, the landscape architect Geoffrey Jellicoe revived the idea of linear megastructures fit into viaducts with his project Motopia, in this case providing a network of rooftop highways intersected by traffic circles every mile and large public gardens tucked into the residual squares. Motopia left the ground plane completely free, but the gardens enclosed by elevated highways would probably have generated a strong sense of claustrophobia. Another effort at combining elevated roads and megastructures arrived with the Japanese Metabolists of the 1960s. Kenzo Tange proposed a grid of elevated highways that would extend across Tokyo Bay, intersected with curving blocks of housing that would hover over the site like docks at a port. For the world's most populous city, this must have seemed a great advantage, as it left the ground plane completely free for landscaping. Alas, the problem with all of these models, in their vision of urban space free of plazas and streets, is that the residual spaces, such as those of Bijlmermeer, outside of Amsterdam, or the Corviale block on the outskirts of Rome, become desolate no-mans-lands.

In the end perhaps the only visually satisfying experiment of infrastructure and linear organization is that of Brasília, the capital city of Brazil planned from 1954 to 1960 by Lucio Costa and filled with the monumental architecture of Oscar Niemeyer. By most accounts, the formal beauty of Brasília's spaces is not sufficient compensation for its lack of urban vitality. The neighborhoods, which are organized in large frames, or *supercuadras,* are functional from the point of view of automobile circulation but do not permit neighbors' paths to cross. Within Brasília, the distances between the government district, the housing areas, and the commercial areas are so large that the residents must use the car for all functions, repeating the same problems that occur in less-planned areas of sprawl. One of the paradoxes of Brasília is that the quality of urban life is more interesting in the illegal outskirt towns that were not governed by the pilot plan. Here one finds mixed-use streets with open markets and gathering spaces. The sublime quality of Brasília is due to its bold scale and unsettling social void. The architectural shells acquire a metaphysical or ghostly quality. Urban visions on this dimension are by their nature totalizing in terms of the programming of space but in most cases are nearly always impossible to realize because of political and financial conflicts, if not sociological regrets. To exploit infrastructure principally for artistic intentions, without allowing for urban intimacy, has rendered Brasília like an enormous sculpture, with few possibilities for the variety of urban life to take over.

The city as infrastructure. Brasilia, Brazil's capital, planned by Lucio Costa, 1954–1960.

From Decoration to Decontextualization

Until the twentieth century, the idea of infrastructure as art was usually regarded as a need for decoration and governed by the classic criterion of "the good, the true, and the beautiful." A work of public art, like a fresco or a sculpture, was always considered additive and not inherent to the functional structure. Among works of infrastructure, the bridge, because of its uniting role, has always engendered critical responses and symbolic interpretations and thus received particular artistic attention. The dialogue between technique and form in bridge making provides the foundation for an eventual theory of infrastructure as art. For instance, for the Rialto bridge in Venice, which burned down in the early sixteenth century, various solutions were considered over a long period. The Classical vision of Andrea Palladio, which placed ornate temple fronts over a three-vault span (temple fronts) that addressed the traffic on the Grand Canal and was rejected by the procurators, probably for the great expense, but also for the ostentation of the decoration. Eventually they chose a more modest proposal by Antonio da Ponte, which was also technically more innovative in that it crossed the canal with a single span. It was less ornate, with only a few pilasters and an understated tympanum at its apex, and its beauty depended less on ostentatious decoration and more on unusual engineering.

During the Industrial Revolution, the explicit use of new technologies was often controversial. Perhaps the most contentious design was for the Forth Bridge at Queensford in Scotland (1873–89). Designed by Benjamin Baker, it was the longest bridge of its time, and its structure of tubular steel members was left completely unadorned. The strange shape of the lattice of the flaring trusses of its cantilevered system was calibrated for spanning strength and wind resistance. A triumph of structural determinism, the Forth Bridge proved to be a sublime work, the nakedness of which prompted critics such as William Morris to see it as "supremely ugly." To dissenters, the engineer responded that "fitness was the fundamental condition of beauty" (Billington 1983). Baker's bridge still transmits a disturbing beauty that is difficult for most to accept.

Other bridges of the period, such as Robert Stephenson's Britannia Bridge (1850) and particularly John A. Roebling and Son's Brooklyn Bridge in New York (1869–83), were more easily recognized as works of art. The Brooklyn Bridge combined conventional decorative devices, such as lancet masonry arches, with the new technical wonder of steel cables for its suspension. Crossing the bridge, poets and painters were inspired by the kinetic effects of the suspension cables, immortalized in the verses of Walt Whitman and Hart Crane. The raw power of the structure gave it instant symbolic primacy for the rising metropolis.

Among the next generation of Manhattan bridges, the case of the George Washington Bridge demonstrates how diffuse the popular understanding of structure as art was. Designed during the 1920s with the collaboration of the Classical architect Cass Gilbert, the steel truss frame of the bridge was intended to be covered with masonry decoration. After the crash of 1929, however, austerity was imposed, while the naked trusses of the structure were thought by the general public to be beautiful and without need of revetment. The work can safely be attributed to its engineer, Othmar Herman Ammann.

The beauty of structural expression and ingenious technical solutions have become important iconic aspects of new urban bridges. The tubular slingshots holding up Norman Foster's Westminster Footbridge (2000) in London, seemed at first to be a triumph of technique over function, since the bridge was initially subject to tremors (which have since been corrected). It gives London's riverfront a new technological imprint to rival the neo-Gothic Tower Bridge (1894) downstream as the symbol of the city. The Erasmus

Westminster Footbridge by Norman Foster, London, 2000.   Ijburg Bridge by Nicholas Grimshaw, Amsterdam, 2002.

Bridge (1996) in Rotterdam, by Ben van Berkel, borrows freely from the structural vocabulary of Santiago Calatrava, presenting a harp-like suspension structure as the gateway to the city, connecting the newly transformed docklands of Kop van Zuid to the center city. It instantly became the symbol of the city. Calatrava's swooping skeletal structure for the Felipe II Bridge (1987), spanning the Bac di Roda train yards of Barcelona, serves a similar purpose of giving an iconic identity to an area of the city that was poorly connected and degraded. Nicholas Grimshaw's Ijsburg Bridge (2000) in Amsterdam reprises Baker's structural solution at Forth in a more sinuous manner. The spectacular structure is meant to attract interest for the new island to be developed over the next decade as an urban nucleus. In all of these cases, the appreciation of structural essentialism, of infrastructure as art, is accepted because of the undisputed functional role of the bridge, allowing it to become a symbol of place and civic life. If the engineering of bridges is conventionally accepted as art, one must inquire why the same criterion is not usually reserved for other works of public utility.

During the twentieth century, aesthetic codes in the arts were upturned. Art was no longer considered a means of representation but, through the various movements based on abstraction and conceptualism, an end in itself. The neo-plasticism of Theo van Doesberg and Piet Mondrian during the 1920s proposed painting as orthogonal lines and pure colored planes capable of suggesting spatial effects. Kasimir Malevich's theory of "Suprematism" further eliminated the role of representation, first presenting a black square on a white background (1913) and later a pure "white square" (1918).

The most destabilizing protagonist of the twentieth-century avant-garde was without doubt Marcel Duchamp, whose concept of the "readymade" threw into doubt the nature of art ever after. The snow shovel, the bottle rack, the immobilized bicycle wheel—all items produced by industrial culture—when removed from their contexts could be contemplated as art. In 1917, Duchamp launched his provocation by entering into the Society of Independent Artists Exhibition in New York a urinal laid on its side, titled *Fountain*. The capsized urinal, full of the sarcasm of a scatological joke, nonetheless opened the way toward a new approach to the sublime. Duchamp, in his inimitable manner, explained readymades as "a complete anesthesia," and from that moment on beauty could be found in the negation of art (Camfield 1989). To emphasize his anti-art position, Duchamp drew whiskers on a reproduction of Leonardo da Vinci's *Gioconda*, adding the cryptically obscene acronym "L.H.O.O.Q." (which when uttered phonetically means "She has a hot bottom"). Duchamp's readymades were proposed as objects of unconscious beauty. Duchamp discovered that instead of reproducing or representing meaning, he could unchain the inherent beauty of things by simply decontextualizing a real object, humble or disgusting as it may have been. His most paradoxical readymade, "Door 11 rue Larrey," was installed in his rooms at rue Larry during the 1920s in Paris. A single door was hinged to two adjacent frames, one to the room and one to the closet, so that when the door was open for one, it was closed for the other. Since Duchamp, much of the discourse of modern art revolves around the negative capacity of decontextualization (Camfield 1989).

During the 1960s, the American artist Robert Smithson became the chief ideologue of a new approach to art that he called "Earthworks" and that critics now call Land Art. Passing through the negative criteria of Duchamp, he taught a generation of artists how to see infrastructure as readymades. In an article for *Art Forum*, Smithson visited his hometown of Passaic, New Jersey, with a Kodak Instamatic, taking tourist snapshots of scenes of industrial degradation as if he were visiting the monuments of Rome (Smithson 1967). Among the suburban *mirabilia* of bridges, sandboxes, parking lots, and pipes, was a set of sluice pipes filling the river with dubious effluents, for which he chose the Duchampian title of *Fountain*. Smithson abandoned all sarcasm in his later research as the artistic consultant to the planners of the Dallas–Fort Worth airport. From that moment on he began to imagine art on a territorial scale, and, although he accomplished nothing for the airport, he found in his musings a method of decontextualizing elements of infrastructure with respect to geographic sites. According to his theory, "One should never impose on the site but rather expose the site." Dams, highways, and airports become readymades at a scale of 1:20,000.

Pop Art and the Play of Scale

During the same years that Smithson opened the way toward Land Art, Claes Oldenburg began to reproduce ironic versions of everyday readymades on a colossal scale. Giant replicas of a fan, a baseball bat, an eraser, and a lipstick were proposed as monuments for public space. One of his more cavalier projects was the unrealized *Thames Ball,* designed in 1967: an enormous set of two balls, balanced on London Bridge, overlooking the Houses of Parliament, resembling the devices that maintain water levels in a toilet. The heritage of Duchamp's *Fountain*

Claes Oldenburg's "Mistos," a colossal pack of matches strewn across the intersection of the Vall d'Hebron olympic area, 1992.

was revived once again on a grand scale. Oldenburg's works have become a conventional way to decorate ironically new infrastructural interventions. For the suburban district of Vall d'Hebron, one of the 1992 Olympic sites in Barcelona, Oldenberg installed *Mistos* (1992), a colossal pack of matches scattered into three corners of an intersection of new roads: in one corner a crumpled match, in the other an erect and lit match as an unlikely version of the Olympic torch. For a large advertising agency in Venice, California, designed in the 1980s by Frank O. Gehry, Oldenberg installed an outsize pair of binoculars as an improbable entryway; in a famously sprawling landscape where one is constantly looking for signs, this sign is something one looks through then eventually walks through. More recently, Oldenberg placed *Needle, Thread, and Knot* in the redesigned Piazza Cadorna in Milan. The ironic reference to the nodal function of the piazza is perhaps a bit overstated. The pop art monuments of Oldenburg are additive works that decontextualize everyday items out of both place and scale.

In the town of Gibellina in Sicily, which was totally rebuilt on a new site in 1968 after being destroyed in an earthquake, a unique program of art added to infrastructure was initiated as a means of compensating for the absence of urbanity and loss of identity after reconstruction. Over the past twenty years, famous artists and architects have participated in creating a cultural patrimony of more public artworks per capita than in any city of the world. The most famous of the works, Alberto Burri's *Il Cretto* (1985–2005), covers the entire site of the defunct old city with a forty-acre, four-foot-deep sarcophagus of concrete. Scored with pathways that recall the street system of the vanished city, *Il Cretto* is a sublimely moving memorial to the death of this city and the city in general. The entry to Gibellina is now marked by Pietro Consagra's *Stella del Belice* (1983), a colossal drive-through star that in a pop art manner recalls the *luminarie* lanterns hung as street decorations during Sicilian urban festivals.

Another case of pop art decoration occurred for the new metro stations in Naples, curated by Alessandro Mendini. The Salvator Rosa stop explodes with images and contrasting colors: a blue obelisk poised on a pyramidal light well, swirling mosaics and outsize flowerpots, cryptic hieroglyphs and sunbursts, and a bronze Pulcinella statue. The decorations are populist, eclectic, and without harmony yet seem to fit the exuberant spirit of Naples perfectly. One proof is that after two years in use there are no signs of vandalism, though the city is overrun with graffiti. Perhaps the best defense against graffiti was to decorate the subway stops as if they had been designed by graffiti artists.

The irony of the pop art of Oldenburg and others is usually self-conscious. Without this sophistication, populist decoration risks becoming kitsch. In Beijing, at the cloverleaf of Siyuan Qiao, the largest of its new highway interchanges one finds an unintentional pop art decoration. In the midst of twenty ramps, twenty-six bridges, and an area that covers 150,000 square feet, four enormous dragons—the symbol traditionally placed at entries, the sort found at every Chinese restaurant in the world—have been laid out in artful flower beds in the lobes of the cloverleaf. Even if they have been placed there without ironic intention, the dragons of Siyuan Qiao, amid the roar of automobiles and exhaust seem the perfect pop art emblem: decontextualized figures that capture the fury of modern traffic.

A drive-through ready-made gateway. Stella del Belice by Pietro Consagra,
New Gibellina, 1983. Siyuan Qiao freeway intersection in Beijing, 1993.

The Metaphysical Landscapes of Luis Barragán

The Mexican architect Luis Barragán created several landscapes during the 1950s and 1960s that, with minimal additions, heighten one's awareness of the beauty of infrastructure. With his colleague the German sculptor Mathias Goeritz, he conceived one of the most memorable highway decorations: the towers of Satélite, a suburb of Mexico City. Built in 1957 and 1958, the five brightly colored towers were placed randomly on a slightly sloping oval traffic median. Ranging from 90 to 150 feet in height and inspired by the medieval tower houses of San Gimignano, the prows of the triangular prisms point toward the central city and are visible (when smog permits) for five miles. The kinetic impact of the cluster of towers engages the dynamic movement of automobiles, evanescent as one arrives from the center but dense and occluded due to their squared-off rears when seen on the return trip. Although one can imagine a variety of functions for the towers, including water reservoirs and antennae, they were designed for purely formal and promotional reasons, meant to attract home buyers to the new subdivision. During the next decade—above all at the time of the 1968 Olympics—they became an instant icon for the entire city.

Most of Barragán's works were built for private clients in the suburbs of Mexico City. The considerable fortune he gained as a developer and architect was tied to the El Pedregal subdivision, built during the early 1950s and among the city's first automobile-based neighborhoods. The streets were four lanes wide and curved, with few intersections and lots of parking. The public gardens of El Pedregal were intended as a picturesque social center, structured on a series of terraces carved out of the volcanic rocks, and decorated with a sculpture of a serpent by Goeritz. After fifty years, the district has lost the aristocratic spaces intended by Barragán; most of the lots have been resubdivided into denser settlement. The park has almost completely disappeared, and all that remains are the abnormally wide and sinuous streets.

Barragán designed two other suburbs in the 1960s, in which he gave almost as much attention to horses, of which he and his clients were enthusiasts, as to cars. The small subdivision of Los Clubes has a central civic element: the Lovers Fountain, a shallow pool framed by interlocking pink planes, over which a water-gushing aqueduct has been cantilevered. Two wooden horse troughs have been propped upright to resemble the lovers. In another subdivision nearby, Las Arboledas (1958–61), horses are trotted along an avenue lined with large eucalyptus trees and flanked by a two-mile-long red wall. This formal element provides a type of unity that is usually missing in edge settlements. At the end of the axis is a grand, thirty-foot-long trough at the end of which, in a staggered position is a fifteen-foot-high colored plane. While the space is wonderfully open, one has a sense of protection and enclosure due to the subtle framing of the colored planes. At the horse ranch of San Cristóbal (Egerstrom House 1967), the barnyard gives a good example of how one could organize urban space. The space is enclosed by magenta- and rose-colored planes, gaps left between them at the corners and square arches cut into them for passageways. In the center is a pond fed by a water-spewing aqueduct, cantilevered over a freestanding plane. The metaphysical atmosphere is sustained by the geometric purity of the planes and the deep shadows they cast.

A highway interchange as a series of rooms by Ricardo Legoretta and Peter Walker, Solana, 1988.

Barragán's metaphysical approach, composing a sequence of semi-enclosed spaces using kinetic juxta-positions of colored planes, was borrowed by his friend Ricardo Legorreta for numerous projects, includ-ing a large highway inter-change at the business park of Solana, thirty miles northwest of Dallas. Designed with landscape architect Peter Walker in 1988, the Solana off-ramps are signaled by eighty-foot-high colored pylons, a yellow one to the south, and a violet one to the north, recalling the towers of Satélite. As one leaves the freeway, one passes through a series of outdoor rooms that have been framed with freestanding colored planes and square arches. The kinetic effects are created through abstract compositions gracefully added to the structure of the highway. The effect of driving through the great rooms is both uncanny and reassuring, a true marker of place.

The Social Integration of Art and Infrastructure in Barcelona

Over the last twenty-five years, Barcelona has carried out a remarkable program of urban renewal, reworking brownfield sites and modernizing infrastructure. The Barcelona model combines a high degree of artistic participation with social programs that serve popular uses. The historical particulars are perhaps unique to Barcelona and cannot be repeated everywhere: after the conclusion of Franco's totalitarian government in 1975, the region of Catalonia regained its linguistic and political autonomy with a socially progressive undercurrent, while a large class of young professionals weaned on Miró and Tàpies were ready to begin their careers. Although the master plan (PGM) of the city had already been approved in 1974, the character of the city changed with a liberated, post-Franco interpretation of the plan. Oriol Bohigas catalyzed the design community with the simple observation that a plan is only as good as the projects designed for it. From 1980 to 1992 he directly influenced the process of remaking Barcelona, first of all firing the old guard instead of the planning agencies, staffing them with fifth year architecture students instead. Every act of infrastructure, from the Cinturón ring-road highway to the new subway stops to renovated plazas to new parks, was treated as an opportunity for art and social improvement. As Bohigas put it:

It is necessary to interrupt the old and counterproductive dichotomy between urbanism and the politics of public works, which has given a schizophrenic tone to the development of our cities. While the urbanists analyzed and planned, looking for a new method to work on the city, the technicians of public works continued to work in the healthy tradition of constructing the city realistically, but without an integrated vision of its areas...or devoting themselves unilaterally to traffic engineering. It is time to approach urbanism with the tools of public works; build an urbanism that is capable of uniting and harmonizing the projects of urbanization. Designing and realizing plazas, streets, boulevards, ramblas, intersections, pedestrian paths, street furniture, street signs, monuments (Bohigas 1986).

The objective of Bohigas's initiatives was to promote a local identity for all of the neighborhoods of the city, or in his words to "sanitize the center and monumentalize the periphery." Along with the attention to technical programs and social needs, the form of the projects was always a major issue. One of the toughest districts in the barrio gótico, the Raval, was partly cleared for a *rambla* connecting to the new cultural district that includes Richard Meier's Museum of Contemporary Art (1987–1995) and Viaplana & Piñon's CCCB cultural center (1990–94). Although the connection has instigated a minimum of gentrification, it is remarkable how the lower classes have resisted in the area. The Parque Miró (1983), which was recuperated from the site of the old slaughterhouses on the southern edge of the barrio gótico, is an early example of the spot clearances in the dense historic center that were designed with a mixture of abstraction and surrealism that infiltrated the iconography of new public works in Barcelona. The antithetical obelisk, based on a drawing by Joan Miró, stands guard over the geometrically organized paved plaza and shady bosque. Other sites in outer districts were designed with sculptural set pieces by Eduardo Chillida, Richard Serra, and Ellsworth Kelly. Each intervention was usually connected with a social amenity such as a school, library, community center, or playing field. Within the span of a generation, the entire city was quite systematically requalified with new parks, bridges, bike paths, plazas, benches, schools, and the miraculous recovery of more than six miles of coastline of the world's finest urban beach.

Bohigas involved a wide range of modern architects and, with his active role as a critic, initiated a "culture of design" aimed both at the architects and the clients. The new spaces generated around infrastructural interventions gave a remarkable new style to the city. Quite often the formal results were stunning. An underlying aesthetic impulse was triggered by the reconstruction of Mies van der Rohe's German Pavilion, originally built for the World Exposition of 1929. The composition was organized according to neo-plasticist sensibilities, an interlocking system of planes made of pure materials: travertine paving, a sheer entry pool, an onyx wall, an opaque glass light trap, full glass panes, and four chrome-covered steel columns with an X section. The single figurative element was Kolbe's bronze nude, placed in the interior reflecting pool. The only anthropometric reference were two of Mies's Barcelona chairs.

The luxurious minimalism of the German Pavilion found its way into many urban projects for Barcelona. The plaza in front of the new central train station, Sants, by Viaplana, Piñon, and Miralles (1981–83), has an eerie metaphysical look related to the austere voids of Mies. It meets the major intersection with skeletal shading devices and is solidly paved in smooth granite (much-loved by the international skateboarders who come like pilgrims to scoot about the site). The pergola stands an ungainly five stories high, propped up on sixteen slender steel columns that are surreally anchored in rounded boots. Next to the pergola, an undulating canopy, made of the same steel palette, sweeps from the front of the plaza to the station entry. In the western corner, two rows of stainless steel tubes squirt water in rhythmically timed bursts to cool the plaza and protect it from the noise and fumes of traffic. The lightness of the elements and the "hardness" of the plaza at Sants station were determined by the structure below it, which had been built to cover the train tracks and could not support great loads or planters, which led to the solution of a series of thin excrescences worthy of the emaciated figures of Alberto Giacometti. The diagrammatic forms of the plaza enclosed

The hard plaza loved by skateboarders. Sants Estacion by Viaplana, Piñon, Miralles, Barcelona, 1983.

the space with ephemeral charm and produced a peculiar style that affected other parks and plazas.

Many districts that are distant from the center have today become genuine civic centers, well equipped with public transportation and social services and truly memorable as urban form: the great canopy of Via Julia (1986–89), the tree-lined rambla of Poble Nou (1989–92). The great projects for recovering brownfield sites, such as the park inserted into the ex-quarry of La Creueta (1981–87) or the park that reused the old train yards of Clot (1982–86), are fine examples of how it is possible to turn the disadvantages left by the old industrial structure of a city into positive places for the recreation and education of citizens in post-industrial times. Both designs have left archaeological evidence of the previous function while inserting playing fields and leisure spaces.

The selection of Barcelona as the host for the 1992 Olympics pushed the scale of urban-renewal operations to a metropolitan level. Choosing four principal sites at relatively far distances (the stadium district of Montjuic, the University City, the western-edge district of Vall d'Hebron, and for the Olympic Village the ex-industrial area of Icaria) created new incentives to complete the ring road of highways and introduce better public-transportation connections. The

Another view of Sants Estacion.

works for the Olympics were treated with the same attention to social investment in neighborhoods, thus yielding new playing fields, parks, and social centers with each infrastructural work. The Cinturón ring road was handled with superb attention to minimizing the negative effects of traffic, cutting and covering the thoroughfare wherever possible and introducing parks as connective tissue where the road had caused a fracture. The coastline park of Poble Nou (1989–92), by Manuel Ruisánchez and Xavier Vendrell, is a splendid cover for three miles of highway between the Olympic Village and the new district of Diagonal Mar. It provides a green filter between the dense housing district and the beach and, in a fanciful manner with rusting bits of maritime detritus and the sculptural treatment of ventilator shafts serving the highway below, produces a picturesque experience that periodically opens the view to traffic.

An even more obvious attempt to exploit the sublime nature of traffic arteries infused the design of La Trinitat park, captured in the center of one of the city's largest traffic interchanges. Designed by Enric Batlle and Joan Roig (1991–92), the park connects to the surface roads of the district and a subway stop. Using the same curves of the elevated highways that frame it, the park contains a layered program that includes a small lake, tennis courts, playgrounds, and an orchard. Despite the good intentions to create at La Trinitat a green filter for the ferocious interchange, the noise, speed, and fumes

Coastline park of Poble Nou by Manuel Ruisánchez and Xavier Vendrell, Barcelona, 1990s.

are frankly overwhelming, and the park's users are somewhat at risk even from the acoustic pollution.

The northwestern range of the Cinturón, known as Ronda de Dalt (1989–92) was handled with magnificent sculptural attention under the guidance of Josep-Anton Acebillo, and the drive from La Trinitat to Vall d'Hebron is animated with fascinating kinetic effects. The walls rise up and step down, sometimes partially covered with curved labia that reach over the highway. At other points, the road is crossed over and punctured with a variety of light wells. Parks cross overhead and canopies thrust toward the road. The great arching pergola of Via Julia is visible as one passes by; a civic center with a library has been artfully stacked on one of the crossovers at Via Favencia by Marciá Codinachs & Mercé Nadal, (1992); the ring-shaped traffic circle of Karl Marx Plaza is suspended gracefully over the highway. The experience of the sublime aroused by highway infrastructure has been artfully integrated into a natural and civic landscape. The Barcelona model signifies the integration of social and aesthetic purposes with the utilitarian programs of public works and a belief that infrastructure can enrich the life and the imagination of the city.

Sense and Consensus

The end of the twentieth century witnessed the greatest demand for new infrastructure. Highway construction and renovation continues unchallenged, with few exceptions, as do new flyovers and parking structures. Hundreds of airports have been rebuilt for expansion and restructuring. New subway lines, intermodal transit stations, and, above all, the high-speed rail lines are causing major changes in the landscape of sprawl. New infrastructures for telematic networks have dotted the urban edge with antennae. Even the underfunded alternative energy plants (photovoltaics and wind) are starting to mark the land. Near most large cities, artificial hillsides—modern ziggurats made of garbage—are changing the topography.

In the neo-liberal context that currently dominates the world economic system, infrastructures are proposed as winning programs for public investment and usually gain public consensus. There are, of course, many dubious projects, such as Italy's plan for the world's largest suspension bridge (over the straits of Messina) that have met with local and international disapproval. Generally, however, new infrastructure is treated as ineluctable and beneficial. When wise resistance fails, it is better to follow the example of Barcelona and try to give a social and aesthetic sense to these expensive and disruptive interventions.

The photovoltaic tower of Forum 2004, Barcelona.

Smithson, in his return to the "negative capacity of art," opened a vision toward the territorial dimensions of infrastructure and its ability to express the poetic allegory of modern times. His most famous work, the *Spiral Jetty* (1971), a coiled landing that juts into the Great Salt Lake, was constructed with the same techniques used to make highways and has a geometry similar to the turning radius of off-ramps. The trucks that brought the landfill produced the road they needed to continue the spiral until they reached the point where they could proceed no further. It was a useless intervention that purposefully disappeared under the rising lake, only to reemerge at moments when the lake subsides.

What Smithson alluded to was that works of infrastructure are readymades waiting to be decontextualized. This does not justify all infrastructures as being inherent works of art, but it does lead to the possibility that infrastructure can be discovered by designers, worked on by them, and framed into a mode of appreciation. Transportation infrastructures continue to be designed with the positivist ethos of government institutions and thus elicit a certain inevitable determinism that corresponds to the economics of increased mobility. Despite their political consensus: these interventions are often upsetting and alienating. Their functional, economical importance affects the culture of cities and needs to be accompanied by an attempt to reinforce a contribution to a sense of community. Citizens and designers could demand more of infrastructure than just its primary function.

Among the memorable acts of resistance to infrastructure was the victorious campaign in 1959 in San Francisco to interrupt the construction of an elevated highway intended to connect the Embarcadero with the Golden Gate Bridge (ironically the section of the highway that was constructed was torn down due to seismic damage in the 1989 earthquake). Jane Jacobs, who initiated the great objections to modernist tabula rasa urban renewal and brought the world's attention to the value of mixed use, led a successful campaign in Manhattan to save part of Greenwich Village from a highway interchange. Yet despite these exceptional cases, it is quite obvious that transportation infrastructures are among the few services that gather a general consensus. Often paid for by the taxes on gasoline, they seem expedient in generating their own financing. In a certain sense, this unopposed progress of infrastructure should be looked at as a resource to exploit. As in Barcelona, the public works can become part of a culture of design.

Even if society continues to support the construction of new roads without much discrimination, when there is a question of infrastructure as art, the matter of style becomes an issue. The case of Richard Serra's ill-fated *Tilted Arc*, a public sculpture commissioned in 1979 for the Federal Plaza in Lower Manhattan and removed ten years later, is instructive. Serra inserted a colossal, nine-foot-high plane of Cor-ten steel, curved and slightly inclined in the middle of an overexposed public plaza. The piece was so large that visitors to the plaza were forced to circumambulate it and in the process discover its peculiar geometry. This parallax play on perception, executed in the austere mode of minimalist abstraction, was not well loved by the bureaucrats working in the government building, mostly because it blocked the shortest path to the restaurants directly in front of their offices, forcing them to walk 150 feet farther. The conceptual beauty of *Tilted Arc* did not correspond to a popular idea of art, and, after a long legal battle, it was removed. Serra designed a similar arc for a park in Barcelona in the 1980s, and it has survived admirably in the different social and cultural context. The difference resides in the promotion of a culture of design, which can make such a work congruent rather than hostile to its setting.

Infrastructures as utilitarian responses to the pressing problems of mobility invariably cause environmental and social problems. To approach infrastructure as art can provide a way of dealing with the violence it interjects into the urban system and become a means of creating civic meaning. A compelling example is Freeway Park in Seattle, designed by Lawrence Halprin in 1976. At the point where the four off-ramps of the interstate freeway plunge into the down-town, an aerial park bridges the ten-lane artery. Built of the same reinforced concrete as the freeway, it is structured on planters for tall sequoia trees and animated by several gushing cascades. The water and trees offer a buffer to neutralize the effects of traffic. At the base of one of the fountains, there is a window that allows one to view the passing traffic. Although the landscape design has a few serious flaws (too many dark corners and an overly complex circulation), it is otherwise a glorious exception to the brutality of freeways in urban sites.

The fact remains that the majority of infrastructural works are conceived without artistic motivation. Beyond the aesthetic approaches, which can range from postmodern decoration in Naples to Smithson's new sublime to the incomprehensibility of *Tilted Arc*, when infrastructure is treated as art, it enforces the idea that a place has meaning. While the utilitarian logic of infrastructure usually condemns it to a single function, urban life would be greatly enriched if, as in Barcelona, infrastructure were complicated with other functions, such as leisure and social life. Infrastructure as art anticipates a different kind of mobility, one that can tolerate a variety of speeds. By decontextualizing functional elements, one can start to imagine rich associations: if Duchamp's urinal had not been turned on its side, it would not have become a "fountain." If automobiles should somehow disappear in the future, or if, as is more likely, their use increases, the indispensable works of infrastructure that integrate artistic and social purposes will endure as civic contributions of lasting value and fulfill the promise of the cathedral of mobility.

Freeway Park by Lawrence Halprin, Seattle, 1976.

5

The Ecology Question
Sprawltown as a Second Nature

Wind farm near Pamplona, Spain, 2002.

The Post-Apocalypse

Over the course of the past three centuries, Western science has invented the technical means of disseminating the Industrial Revolution. It has not been as successful in inventing remedies of undoing the subsequent damage that industrial civilization has wrought. The current environmental situation, despite all of the indications of greater well-being, is frankly terrifying. The calculations of ecological catastrophe have surpassed all precedents and leave little promise or time for applying correctives. The global greenhouse effect, the melting of the polar ice caps and alpine glaciers, the rising of the levels and temperatures of the oceans, the imbalance of ecosystems, and the severe changes in the climate are linked to anthropogenic causes. Biodiversity is visibly declining; every year one notices fewer sparrows and frogs. During the last fifty years, thirty to fifty percent of animal species have become extinct. A few specialists are ready to include *homo sapiens* among endangered species due to wars, terrorism, famine, and environmental degradation (Rees 2003).

If in 1970, thirty-five percent of the world's population lived in urban situations, the percentage has recently surpassed fifty percent and is projected to be seventy-five percent in another two generations. Many countries, including the U.S., Japan, and the U.K., as well as Mexico and Venezuela, have already surpassed that proportion (d'Andrea 2000). The ecology question is intimately tied to the urban question. The city, the most glorious of mankind's products, continues to grow and invade the world as sprawl. Its low-density, horizontal spread makes it increasingly dependent on fossil fuels. The urban setting produces the majority of greenhouse gases. Urban development is the most critical factor in the planetary crisis, and thus the ecology question should be asked in terms of urban life.

What can be done? There are three major ideological trends in confronting the environmental crisis: 1) "deep ecology," according to which nature, and not humans, should be given priority and first rights; 2) green lobbies that seek protective legislation, green incentives for alternative energy sources, and new technological remedies to reform the situation; and 3) social ecology, which proposes that green solutions are social issues to be resolved through participation. These approaches range from misanthropism to permissivism to idealism, and although there have been isolated instances of success, none of the three has yet to maintain a lasting political impact.

On the planetary level, the first document prepared for the United Nations with respect to the care of environmental patrimony was for a meeting in Stockholm in 1972. Only in 1987, with the Montréal Accords, however, was a clear program of international action set forth in the agenda to eliminate the release of CFCs (chlorofluorocarbons), accompanied by the rather unrealistic goal of reducing greenhouse gases fifty percent over the following ten years. The meeting in Rio de Janeiro in 1992 resulted in Agenda 21, a guideline for sustainable development that continues to have wide circulation among local governments. The negotiations are still proceeding to ratify the 1997 Kyoto Protocol for the reduction of greenhouse gases to eight percent below the levels of 1990. Thus far, 123 nations have signed, including all of the members of the European Union, while both the U.S. and Russia, two of the world's most significant polluters, continue to hold out, making the effects of the treaty at this point a question of voluntary application. The last meeting of U.N. delegates, in Johannesburg in 2002, concluded with bitter regrets about the coordination of international controls. The good intentions in Kyoto will remain mere palliatives until there is a concerted effort to coordinate international with local initiatives.

Melting glaciers in Switzerland, 2002.

Among the more optimistic outcomes of social ecology has been the invention of the Social Forum, founded in 2001 at Porto Alegre in Brazil. More than five thousand delegates from 117 countries met to compare methods of self-organization and sustainability. Members of cooperatives, nongovernmental organizations (NGOs), and cultural associations presented cases for a general strategy, known as "no global," to oppose the impact of neoliberal policies, vacuous consumerism, and the degrading effects that globalization has been contributing to society and the environment. The Social Forum of Porto Alegre is repeated every year and has been exported to other contexts, including Florence, Paris, and Boston, with the mission to put into practice E. F. Schumaker's slogan from the 1970s: "Think global. Act local."

There are those who, when confronted with the environmental crisis, advocate turning back to supposedly simpler times. The urbanist Leon Krier, for instance, proposes to return to a city that is the morphological and social equivalent of the pre-industrial age. But this seems particularly unreasonable since the mythical autarky of the past and the way people today are living and working in an ever more diffused and interdependent manner are in total contradiction. A change in urban form will not necessarily lead to a change in a way of life. The neo-villagers of Poundbury (the model neighborhood in Dorchester designed by Krier and funded by the Prince of Wales, from 1988 to 1996), in order to pay for their pre-industrial–style cottages, will probably continue to work in distant places, such as London, and to shop in the hypermarkets of sprawl. While the setting looks as if it were able to stop sprawl, the economy of its participants is inevitably ensnarled with it. It is in fact much more difficult to move backward than to move forward.

One of the most pervasive responses to the ecology question is forms of prohibition. Could the success of "no smoking" be applied to an urban territory? The triumph of "no smoking," which started locally and became an international movement, is indeed a serious model, but the urban situation has more contentious economic consequences when it involves the fumes of smokestacks and exhaust pipes. To propose controls usually implicates matters of justice, authority, and application that are complicated by formidable conflicts of interest.

In Thomas More's *Utopia*, published in 1516, one can find the germ of the problem plaguing the environmental movement: despite all of the good intentions and great needs, a regime based on ecology will probably not have much need for the project of individual liberty. In *Utopia*, the distribution of resources is decided on a regional level; the division of labor and the control of growth are handled with strict regulation. All citizens must work in agricultural production for two years of their lives and during each year must participate for brief periods when needed. The citizen cannot own his house but instead is obliged to change houses every ten years so as not to begin to feel too proprietary. All of the houses are the same, practical design. All of the fifty-four cities of Utopia are the same plan, each twenty-five miles from the next, each with controlled growth set at about sixty thousand inhabitants. The needs of each neighborhood of thirty houses are collectivized, the matron of each house cooking for the entire neighborhood once a month. There was no money or private property in Utopia, no luxury, all clothing unadorned and uniform.

The model society described by More was inspired directly by his four-year stay in a Carthusian monastery. In retrospect, many of the peculiarities of this fictional society seem to have been adopted by Maoist China during the Cultural Revolution, when intellectuals were sent to work the fields. While Utopia eliminates the sources of crime, envy, and vanity, it does not tolerate dissent or any form of individualism. There is universal well-being and no poverty, but there is also totalitarian control over the lives and movements of the inhabitants. Utopia can be seen as a perfectly sustainable, steady-state system; inflexible as the monastic orders, it was incapable of allowing differences and accepting change. Quite often the remedies for a more ecological way of life imply similar authoritarian solutions, an "eco-fascism" born on the shores of Utopia.

Two hundred years ago, the world outside great cities was mostly organized in a system of villages lived in by peasants. When we speak of returning to a more sustainable way of life, however, who among us is willing to return to the hard labor and low status of those times? Consumerism has proved too seductive as the project of modern life. Even if an ecological criterion could successfully penetrate the consumerist system with "bio" products and optimistic recycling campaigns, consumerism is so all-encompassing and saturated that it renders inconsequential any reforming mechanism.

On the other hand, the time may have already passed when the world's resources were sufficient for its way of life. Currently the inhabitants of the U.S. consume about double the resources that Europeans do. The estimated "ecological footprint" of an American—that is, the amount of land necessary to provide for resources and refuse collection—is currently 5.2 hectares (about 12 acres), compared with 3 hectares per European, and .38 per Indian. As has been noted for more than thirty years, the six percent of the world's population that lives in the U.S. consumes more than thirty percent of the world's resources. If all of the inhabitants of the world lived like Americans, the world would need five times its land mass to satisfy their needs. After the Kyoto Accords of 1997, it was determined that the U.S. is the single greatest producer of greenhouse gases, contributing thirty-seven percent. One cannot participate in consumer society without feeling guilty about the environment, but until now the ecology guilt trip has not been capable of shifting the economic power of consumerism toward a politics of sustainability. On the other hand, while the ecology crisis is alarming, it would be counterproductive to succumb to panic. To be extorted by a sense of guilt and of fear for the future ecological apocalypse recalls the worst tactics perpetrated by religions and notions of the afterlife. In a certain sense, if one rationally considers the cumulative effects of Hiroshima, Chernobyl, the holes in the ozone over Antarctica, and the countless environmental traumas that have occurred during the twentieth century, it would not be too preposterous to conclude that the ecological apocalypse has already occurred. Nature, according to Bill McKibben, has not been able to survive the Industrial Revolution, and "the way of life of one part of the world in one half-century is altering every inch and every hour of the globe"(McKibben 1989). As suggested in Andrei Tarkovsky's enigmatic film *Stalker* (1979), the world has become a strangely contested and damaged zone in which its inhabitants wait around in a sort of postapocalyptic malaise.

To admit that the ecological demise of the planet has already happened might help in converting the guilt-trip strategies of environmentalism into something more humane. By analogy, it could be somewhat like being cured of cancer. Wary of the illness metaphor, which Susan Sontag finds saturated with ideas of guilt and recrimination, one might find inspiration in the figure of the cancer survivor, who can be cured and resume a normal life after intense therapy and regular controls. The ex-patient hopes to have vanquished the risk of metastasis but carries the full knowledge that one can never turn back or start anew (Sontag 1977). Dealing with cancer is a bit like recognizing the theory of entropy, by which the degeneration of material and energy can proceed in one direction only. Thus, if one accepts having survived the environmental apocalypse, that it is behind and not in front of us, guilt, self-loathing, and anxiety are no longer needed as the psychological tactics for mustering solidarity. Instead of the futile campaign to redeem the world from environmental ills, the post-apocalypse survivors can seek sustainable therapies, mechanisms of slowing entropy that will allow for a dignified end.

Until now, the ecological guilt trip has been one of the most important tactics for mobilizing public opinion. Despite the growing awareness of sustainability and the promotion of reforming programs, such as the U.N.'s Agenda 21, it is clear that the remedies that have been applied have not been sufficient to slow down the accelerated entropy of the second half of the twentieth century, and it is quite dangerous to deny this fact. Bjorn Lomborg, for instance, in his negation of the ecological catastrophe, provides a cynical rebuttal to the gloomy prognosis:

We are not running out of energy or natural resources. There will be more and more food per head of the world's population. Global warming, though its size and future projections are rather unrealistically pessimistic, is almost certainly taking place, but the typical cure of early and radical fossil fuel cutbacks is way worse than the original affliction, and moreover its total impact will not pose a devastating problem for our future (Lomborg 2001).

Perhaps he means the "near" future. While Lomborg refutes the statistics of ecological doomsayers, the waters have been measurably rising and global temperatures continue to augment with disastrous climatological incidents. Violent weather is averaging $100 billion in damages annually. The minimum of therapy proposed in the Kyoto Protocol would reduce greenhouse emissions by 5.2 percent by 2012. The American reluctance to sign the treaty, under both the Clinton and Bush administrations, shows a persistent spirit of denial. One reason the U.S. opposes the treaty is because developing countries, such as China and India, are not subject to the same controls. Per capita Chinese contribute ten percent as much as Americans, but, taken as a whole population, China is the second greatest contributor to the greenhouse effect.

For the moment, in the country that has contributed the most to the ecology crisis, self-control is the most important method being practiced. Conscientious corporations such as Whirlpool, 3M, Toyota, Sunoco, United Technologies, and Lockheed Martin, have voluntarily adopted the Kyoto Protocol to reduce emissions. Some states, such as California, have introduced legislation to reduce greenhouse gases. In 2002, the city of Seattle was able to meet the terms of the treaty in reducing emissions by reforming public services and the municipal electric company. Despite these efforts, the American production of greenhouse gases has grown much more than predicted since 1997. While, in Germany, emissions have been reduced by nineteen percent, in the U.S., they have increased twenty-nine percent! The president of the European Commission, Romano Prodi took this position:

Some say that the Kyoto Protocol is not fair because it excludes developing countries. But clearly we of the industrialized world, as the ones who have caused the problem, must be the first to offer a solution. Is it fair that the emissions of the U.S. are ten times those of the developing countries (Prodi 2001)?

During the nineteenth century, Friedrich Engels proposed that the "housing question" would become the central issue in the class struggle. Today one might predict that the "ecology question" will take that role in the political struggles of the future. As Amory Lovins puts it, the more the ecological situation worsens, the more renewable resources and environmental quality will be recognized as forms of "natural capital" (Hawken, Lovics, and Lovins 1999). Thus, in the near future, the economic and political agenda will be geared to protecting this capital: 1) by recognizing the economic benefits of the conservation of matter and energy and demanding "resource productivity"; 2) by treating industries with a biological paradigm, or "biomimicry," as if they were like natural organisms; 3) by treating consumer goods as services rather than private property; and 4) by investing in renewable sources of energy.

The energy blackouts in California in 2002 and in London and all of Italy in 2003—aside from the political reasons—illustrate the general absence of strategies for responsibly coordinating resources. The growing scarcity of water resources throughout the world underlines the fact that natural resources are like capital, and the control of these resources (not just of petrol) will be the key to managing the post-apocalyptic context.

Architecture and Nature

Ecology is a relatively new term, invented by the German follower of Darwin, Ernst Haeckel, in 1866. Derived from the Greek word *oikos*, or "house," it comprehends the theory of the interdependence of all organisms in nature. Ecology had instant political implications, including those of its progenitor, who founded the Monist League based on his ideas of the innate pacifism of natural history. If men would observe the laws of nature, Haeckel claimed, and would accept their place in the great complexity of ecosystems, a harmonious state would emerge. Unfortunately, such a theory led quickly to notions of social darwinism and eventually to the racist ideologies of the Third Reich (Bramwell 1989). Aside from his brilliant scientific research, Haeckel was a gifted draftsman. His illustrated treatise, *Kunstformen der Natur* (late nineteenth century) was a masterpiece of graphic art, each plate providing finely detailed visions of the morphology of species. His views of microscopic organisms opened a new world of visual fantasy. The aesthetic influence of his widely circulated treatise was almost as important as the philosophical impact of monism.

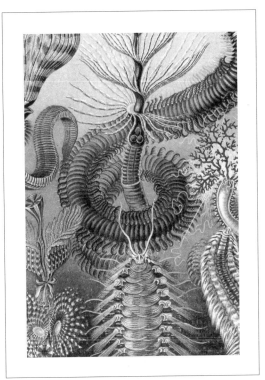

From Ernst Haeckel's *Kunstformen der Natur*, 1899.

Haeckel's greatest interpreter and highly motivated biographer was Rudolf Steiner, a thinker and activist whose ideas are still quite prominent in discussions of ecology. Like Haeckel, Steiner had both a scientific and aesthetic mode of working, which in this case crossed over into architecture. After breaking off from the mystical society of the theosophists, Steiner founded his own school of thought, anthroposophy, in which he combined the ideas of Goethe, Nietzsche, and Haeckel in search of a new spirituality. With his followers, he set up an ideal community in Dornach, Switzerland, where he could test his notions of biodynamic agriculture, organic architecture, and spiritualism. His ideas were brought together in the double-domed, wooden structure of the first Goetheanum (1913–19), which, after its destruction by arson, was rebuilt in reinforced concrete (1921–25) as the greatest project of architectural expressionism of the period. Designed according to the impulses of "spiritual functionalism," the second Goetheanum was Steiner's attempt to synthesize the genius of nature, avoiding all right angles and sculpting the structure in polyhedral forms that echoed the plants, shells, and mineral formations of the Alpine landscape.

Although Steiner is still revered as a prophet of ecologism in the political realm, his ideas, like those of Haeckel, are more often appropriated by the exponents of authoritarianism. The first "biodynamic" farms to be established through state intervention were placed in proximity to the Nazi concentration camps by nature enthusiasts Walther Darré and Alwin Seifert. That ecologism can easily become the tool of totalitarian ideologies is historically grounded and should not be underestimated. The good intentions of the defenders of nature are not always in harmony with concepts of human liberty.

A tendency toward ecology is quite strong in the thought and work of two major protagonists of modern architecture: Le Corbusier and Frank Lloyd Wright (Fernández Galiano 1991). Le Corbusier, born in a town not far from Steiner's anthroposophist community in Dornach, was in the years 1907 to 1915 an enthusiastic participant in a local version of art nouveau based on the stylization of nature. His first chalets are covered with abstracted natural motifs and fit into the topography like natural forms. During the 1920s, after his move to Paris, Le Corbusier completely abandoned the imitation of nature and took up the cause of industrial civilization with slogans such as "The house is a machine for living in." Despite his fame as a technophile, Le Corbusier, after the horrors of World War II and Hiroshima, returned to natural solutions and forms. Almost all of his late projects have green roofs; natural-ventilation slots, which he called *aerateurs*, and built-in *brise-soleil* sunscreens. Perhaps his most famous work, the church of Notre Dame du Haut at Ronchamp (1954), is neither stylistically nor geographically far from Steiner's Goetheanum. The church integrates the natural forces of rain, wind, and sun and demonstrates an architectural expressionism inspired by natural forms. In Le Corbusier's much-published urban model, the *Ville radieuse* (1922–35), which in some drawings he referred to as the "green city," he densely concentrated the dwellings in tall structures in order to leave the majority of the ground plane free for nature. By abandoning the tradition of corridor streets and dense urban patterns, the city could have gardens everywhere. Today, after many applications of Le Corbusier's model, it is difficult to claim that it is an ecologically correct solution because of the prejudices of style and the social stigma attached to the forlorn towers in the park of modernist housing. But one must admit that the vertical concentration of urban functions is potentially more efficient for distribution of services and more respectful of nature than the low-density typologies that sprawl across the land. Historically, the problem with the *Ville radieuse* has been both a lack of coordination of the landscape among the buildings, which has almost always been commandeered by automobile infrastructures, and an absence of urban gathering spaces to support social life.

Frank Lloyd Wright was an even more adamant environmentalist. He called his general approach "organic architecture," by which he meant that buildings should be integrated with nature. His most famous work, *Fallingwater* (the Kaufmann House, 1937), sits atop a waterfall in rural Pennsylvania, and although it could never be analyzed as environmentally efficient, it remains the icon of blending architecture with nature. Wright's most efficient work in terms of sustainability, is the second Jacobs House in Minnesota (1947), a building organized as a solar hemicycle, glazed and open on the south and rooted in a grassy thermal collector berm on the north for passive solar heating.

Like Le Corbusier, Wright produced an ideal vision of the city, a "disappearing city" that would spread across America without urban concentration. His *Broadacre City* (1935) was composed mostly of detached dwellings like the Jacobs House, known collectively as Usonian houses, each of which was allotted a half acre of land, to be worked as orchards or gardens. *Broadacre City* is probably the first aesthetic vision of what American sprawl could become. In this proposal to de-urbanize, the proliferation of highways and high-tech transportation and the mass use of automobiles supported by flying saucers would allow the city to disappear into natural greenery. His individualistic idea that every house could maintain its autonomy and be self-sufficient is quite the opposite of Le Corbusier's collectivized apartment-based solution. While *Broadacre City* was in theory closer to nature, it is quite similar to the suburban solution of the U.S. today, which has proven to be anything but ecologically efficient in its distribution of services, and its increased demands on territorial resources are wasteful.

Although many modernist architects during the 1920s and 1930s were keenly devoted to the research of thermal efficiency and other techniques that would today be called "sustainable," the first time the word *ecology* entered architectural discourse was with Richard Neutra in the 1950s. An Austrian protégé of Loos and Mendelsohn, Neutra immigrated to the U.S. in the mid-1920s and became a disciple of Wright. After settling in Los Angeles, he designed numerous private residences that experimented with a natural equilibrium by following the proper sun orientation, incorporating adjustable shading devices, and employing natural ventilation by means of downdrafts off ponds of water.

Although it is regretted by most environmentalists, who see it only as the source of arid urban situations, modernism should not be underestimated in its concept of sustainable urban design. The research on solar architecture begun at the Bauhaus, crossed over to American house designers such as Keck and Keck, and continued in the later work of Le Corbusier. During the Weimar period in Germany, the landscape architect Leberecht Migge, a consultant to Ernst May and other modernist advocates of the housing movement, integrated the ecological experience with the notion of start-up houses. His *die wachsende Siedlung* (1932), "the unit that grows," involved a basic dwelling with services that could be extended through sweat equity and grow along with the extension of an adjacent orchard to supply a family's needs. This theory was implemented in a few experiments in Frankfurt, but it did not lead to lasting agricultural production, and most of the allotments were sold off. Aside from the exceptional cases of some social-housing estates, such as Neubuhl (1929) in Zurich, the idea of sustainable architecture has in modern times usually been a luxury, geared less to an economic need than to the spiritual needs of the patrons to obtain a more natural lifestyle. The current challenge in the quest for sustainability is to reorient the discourse of sustainability to economic need, allowing for the spiritual benefits to follow it.

Sustainability and Design

The environmental movement entered into political life first in the U.S. during the tumultuous years of the 1960s. With the critique launched by Rachel Carson in *The Silent Spring* (1961), the protest against the atomic bomb, the campaigns for civil rights, the student battles, a new constituency for an environmental lobby took shape. The Sierra Club, which was founded in San Francisco in 1890 and was influential in founding the first national parks, began to mobilize public opinion about the environmental crisis in the 1960s and was followed by a more militant organization, the Friends of the Earth, in the 1970s. The first laws for the defense of endangered species were passed in the U.S. in 1966. After the success of the first Earth Day in 1971, programs for recycling and tree planting were widely implemented. With the energy crisis of 1972–73, many industrialized nations produced laws on thermal efficiency that made a significant impact on energy use. In 1974, President Carter had solar panels installed on the White House to heat the swimming pool (they were later removed by President Reagan). During the 1970s, many activist organizations, such as Greenpeace, Worldwatch Institute, and the World Wildlife Fund, emerged in defense of the environment. In Europe during the same years, ecology started to become a serious political catalyst. In Germany the Green Party was founded in the late 1970s, and by 1987, after the nuclear accident at Chernobyl, was able to take eight percent of the national vote. Even if the Greens in Germany have lost some of their following, they initiated a process that spread to other European countries, where the Green agenda began to infiltrate all legislative discussions. Every political party has begun to use Green rhetoric when it comes to matters of environmental policies.

The field of architecture responded relatively slowly to the politics of the ecology question. The first ecology-oriented architects were sympathizers of Rudolf Steiner. The great quests of the 1960s had resuscitated Utopian and spiritualist tendencies. In Holland in the 1980s, for instance, a firm believer in Steiner's philosophy, Ton Alberts, designed the most energy-efficient office building in

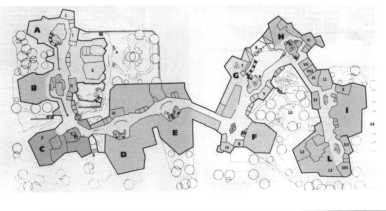

The most energy efficient building in Europe in the 1990s. Arcosanti, Sonoran Desert, Arizona, 1967-2005; NMB (now ING) Bank by Ton Alberts, Amsterdam, 1980s.

Europe. The NMB bank (now ING bank) in the Bijlmermeer suburb of Amsterdam is a bizarre cluster of irregularly shaped towers fit with solar devices, water recycling, naturally enhanced lighting, and sound-deflecting geometries. The weird expressionist shapes of battered walls and polygonal rooms have been explained in terms of sustainable functionality but in their rejection of right angles verge on Steiner's spiritual functionalism.

Paolo Soleri, an Italian architect who came to Arizona to work with Frank Lloyd Wright, was inspired by the ideas of ecology and social communitarianism of the 1960s and attempted to project a synthesis of an ecological worldview with architectural form, a synthesis that he called "archology." His proposals of beehive-like monoliths for metropolitan-scale populations, christened with apocalyptic names such as Novanoah and Babelnoah, were fascinating visions of a neoprimitive and high-tech future. Over the past forty years, in the middle of the Sonoran desert, with the help of volunteer student labor, Soleri has been constructing a model city, Arcosanti, which is intended as an architectural representation of a more compact way of life that could stop sprawl and provide a sustainable system for collective existence. The Utopian premise and political impracticality of Soleri's experiment have been glossed over by a collective enthusiasm to build a full-scale sand castle.

Geodesic dome by R. Buckminster Fuller for the U.S. pavilion, 1967 Expo, Montreal.

A more influential alternative to the mystical tendencies and voluntarism of the 1960s came with the high-tech models of R. Buckminster Fuller. According to Fuller, the problem was not consumerism per se but the great waste of potential in materials and energy resulting from technological inefficiencies. His metaphor for the planet,

"Spaceship Earth," was taken to heart by the environmental movement. His theories of a "dymaxion" world, based on the maximizing techniques of geodesic domes and tensegrity structures had broad appeal, especially to the military, which became his first serious client. But the ideas also appealed to hippies and were used by the anarchic group that built Drop City, Colorado (1968) as a series of geodesic domes made of abandoned automobile carcasses. Steve Baer has continued to refine self-build technologies in the desert with his energy-efficient Zomes. The obsession with recycling car parts for ecology-conscious buildings has been pursued zealously by Michael Reynolds in what he calls "Earthships," built mostly of stacked automobile tires and adobe.

The most celebrated acolyte of Fuller is Norman Foster, who has established a niche in architectural culture for very costly high-tech structures with ecological pretensions. London's new municipal buildings on the Thames have been presented as bio-climatic. Like a daunting, glass-covered beehive, its hemispherical form is tilted to shade the southern exposure and has a central atrium that is a shaft for natural ventilation. It was recently surpassed by the more harmonious conical tower for the RE insurance company (2003). Located in central London, the spiraling structure alternates planted landings that provide natural filters for the forced air. Despite the energy savings of high-tech buildings, there is always the doubt that the high cost of construction will be amortized by its energy performance.

Other strangely shaped projects inspired by Fuller have recently appeared in the name of ecology. One example is the series of bubbles for the Eden Project botanical gardens in Cornwall by Nicholas Grimshaw (2001). Each of the domes rests on a polyhedron lattice supporting a new type of translucent resin. Each protects a different biotic category of garden in an area that was recuperated from a clay quarry. In Phoenix, Arizona, Will Bruder, an ex-follower of Soleri, used Fuller's tensegrity ideas to create the most energy-efficient public building in the U.S., the Central Public Library (1995). On the southern facade are colossal computer-driven Venetian blinds that open and close according to need; the northern facade is festooned with twisting Teflon sails that protect the glass elevation from sun and wind.

The most energy efficient public building in the USA of the 1990s. Phoenix Central Library by Will Bruder, 1995.

High tech is very expensive and requires highly specialized construction. In the 1970s, there was much discussion of "appropriate technology" as an alternate strategy for solutions suitable to local climates and resources. The idea gathered around the work and thought of Egyptian architect Hassan Fathy, who advocated a return to vernacular building methods in order to revitalize local building crafts and include the poorer sectors of the population, who were being marginalized by modernization. Appropriate technology now belongs to various spheres of development, from the self-build edges of Brazilian metropoles to the conscientious architecture in developed countries. Among the best examples of the last ten years are the works of Australian architect Glenn Murcutt, German architect Thomas Herzog, and American architect Sam Mockbee. Murcutt employs an architectural language inspired by the minimalism of Mies van der Rohe, with the difference that every aspect of design is calculated to assist solar energy, natural ventilation, and the recuperation of rainwater. Herzog uses wood and glass with a similar elegance and sustainable performance. Mockbee, with his students and Rural Studio, concocted self-help structures for needy families in the rural South. Using unconventional materials such as recycled fruit cases, bales of hay, blocks of recycled cartons, and carpet samples, he patched together several stunning minimalist dwellings.

Whether it is with high tech, appropriate technology, or traditional methods of construction, architects have no lack of models of sustainability. Yet the professions and industries are slow as ever in responding to real needs without pressing financial incentives.

Redesigning Cities with Bioregional Criteria

To be "ecologically correct" in design can only partially help to confront the problems of the ecological imbalance. The greater concern is how to deal with the city. Of what use are energy savings in a sustainable house if the occupants must continue to use the automobile on the average of nine times per day? To restructure the urban system with bioregional criteria should command all priority. Bioregionalism was first proposed by the Scottish biologist and planner Patrick Geddes and refers to the proper distribution of people to resources in a comprehensive geography that could be considered an ecosystem (Welter 2002). In a state of nature, resources are maintained rather than exploited, organisms adapt to the environment rather than resisting or changing it. In the case of a geographic region, one that can be seen as a natural system, there is no need for the arbitrary political boundaries of city, province, or state. Geddes was nonetheless an apologist for British and French colonialist policies in that he felt they better protected the needs of the land. According to the logic of bioregionalism, urbanization should follow nature's order.

Perhaps the most lasting effort to apply bioregionalism to urbanism came with the Garden City movement begun by Ebenezer Howard, a contemporary of Geddes. Howard's book, *Tomorrow, a Peaceful Path to Real Reform*, published in 1898, attracted a wide following and to this day is the theoretical basis of most green alternatives for city planning. Howard, with his architect associates Unwin and Parker, founded the first Garden City in 1904 at Letchworth as an example of how to contain the oil-stain growth of London. Garden Cities were organized as polynuclear settlements, meant to relieve the pressure from a single center. They were redolent of parks and gardens, thus offering the primary attraction to new dwellers, fixed in terms of their size, and meant to interact with other satellite cities. The land between cities would be maintained in perpetuity as green belts.

The first Garden City was not an economic success but nonetheless left its imprint on urbanism: the super-block and the cul-de-sac made their debut in Letchworth and would condition most of the suburbs built in the latter half of the twentieth century. Instead of becoming the basis of what Howard called the "social city," a polynuclear network of towns connected with good rail transportation, the Garden City became an aestheticized lifestyle, associated with the detached house and garden. In 1946, however, with the New Towns Act for England, Howard's polynuclear "satellite" system was revived and exercised the strongest control on postwar development. Eight new towns were founded approximately twenty to thirty-five miles from the center of London, following the objectives of Howard's social city and to some extent preserving the rural conditions between the towns (Hall and Ward 1998).

Probably the most thorough example of bioregionalist planning has occurred in the region most threatened with political disruption. In Palestine during the 1920s, the Zionist colonists established a series of agricultural villages, the *kibbutzim*, now numbering 270, which were vaguely modeled on Garden City prototypes, for settlements of a hundred to a thousand inhabitants. Geddes came to Palestine from India in the early 1920s to consult on the master plan of Jerusalem, but the Garden City planning of the *kibbutzim* can be attributed to a single designer, Richard Kauffmann, a member of the German Garden City movement. His plan for the cooperative village of Nahalal (1922) is almost a direct transposition of Howard's radiocentric diagram, illustrating the concept of the Garden City. After 1948, his territorial vision was regulated by the realities of the military strategies of the new state of Israel: it is difficult to speak of bioregional order when the political and military order have precedence.

Another exceptional example of bioregional planning occurred in the five new towns for the Agro Pontino between Rome and Naples, built during the major campaign to turn the swamps into farms. During the 1930s, hundreds of settlers were from Po Valley in the north, where similar land reclamations had already been enacted. The new Fascist towns were placed approximately fifteen miles from each other. Sabaudia, designed in modernist style, still demonstrates an ideal relationship between urban fabric and natural surroundings.

The settlement for 5,000 is compact, and the streets are lined with buildings; but its urban blocks are porous and redolent of green spaces, and the edges of the town are well defined by protected greens belts, a lake, and a ten-mile forest.

More recently, in the lands reclaimed from the Zuidersee in Holland, the town of Almere has been organized according to Howard's criteria. Founded in the early 1970s for an eventual population of 250,000 Almere has three urban nuclei, several housing settlements, and protective green belts strategically placed so that it is never more than a ten-minute walk to a natural setting. The question of state ownership of the land greatly facilitated the process of control.

The Garden City ideal is generally quite difficult to implement on the regional scale because of competing political and economic interests. The many derivatives, such as Radburn, New Jersey (1929), usually met with the fate of amalgamation with the unforgiving suburban sprawl that compromised their principles. Within the neoliberal frame, the prospects of implementing sustainable urbanism are fairly confined to local initiatives and voluntarism. A good example of how to deal with a piece of a city remains BedZED

BedZED housing by Bill Dunster, London, 2001.

(Beddington Zero Emission Development, 2001) an urban block of brownfield recuperation built in Hackbridge, an edge district of London. Designed by Bill Dunster Architects, the project combines new techniques of insulation, energy efficiency, and water recycling with social innovations. A relatively high density has been obtained through the row-house type, to which lofts for business or work have been added to provide the possibility of live-work situations. Green roofs, hothouses, and southern terraces improve the environmental performance. All of the building materials, from bricks, and lumber to electrical wiring, were obtained within a thirty-mile radius of the development. The occupants can enroll in a car-sharing program, which boasts forty electric vehicles fueled by photovoltaic energy. BedZED has probably reduced the individual's ecological footprint by half (Buchanan 2002). If the benefits of this urban block could be reproduced city-wide, a sustainable city would begin to emerge.

The Garden City had wide influence. Even Le Corbusier's *La Ville Radieuse* (1935), although it would seem to be the opposite of the folksy look of Howard's Letchworth, was conceived as a vertical Garden City, aspiring to the same ideal land conservation. More recently, the Garden City has returned as a model for the New Urbanism movement led by Andrés Duany and Elizabeth Plater-Zyberk. Addressing the particular conditions of American sprawl, they have outlined ways of preserving open land and reorienting urban development through a set of codes that achieve a mixture of functions and coordinated facades and streetscapes (Duany 2000). Their colleagues Peter Calthorpe and Douglas Kelbaugh have emphasized transportation centers, places in the suburbs to which people can walk in ten minutes to find good connections to the urban transportation system. To reconceive of sprawl as a network of "pedestrian pockets," each centered around a transportation node, would greatly reduce the reliance on the automobile and would create new foci of urban density, like Howard's polynucleated social city. In the 1990s, the Portland metropolitan region implemented a series of transportation centers along its revived lightrail system, demonstrating the positive effect of such planning. Some of these centers have become places of centrality, where cars can be left to shift to other forms of internodal travel. It has given the city options, above all that of going on foot (Calthorpe 1993).

Many European cities are restructuring their transportation systems, reviving the old tram lines. Cities in Switzerland, such as Zurich and Berne, never abandoned their tram systems and show how urban development can be handled in harmony with public transportation. They have expanded with a series of urban nuclei resembling a cluster of grapes. Trams slow urban traffic, and, although this may not be consistent with modernity's desire for greater speed, the calming of traffic is beneficial to urban quality of life. Lyons, France, is among the many cities that has reintroduced light rail with coordinated parking lots, greatly reducing automobile traffic.

Since 1965, the large Brazilian city of Curitiba, population 1.6 million, has offered a unique model of an integrated program of sustainability. The street system was reordered into five "privileged arteries" for public transportation, using buses as efficiently as subways at a current capacity of 1.3 million rides per day. The preferential corridors for buses are served by a series of integrated transportation centers and a related pedestrian network that links to social amenities.

Revising transportation for more nonautomobile options is without a doubt the highest priority in reforming urban regions toward sustainability. In the case of Freiburg, in southern Germany, planning measures for renewable sources of energy have been coordinated with good mass transit and bike paths to create a "solar region." Over the past decade, the city and region have promoted the production and installation of photovoltaic systems, reducing the local emission of

Integrating sustainable practices for the solar region. Freiburg, Germany.

greenhouse gases by twenty-five percent. More than 450 businesses for alternative energy production have been generated, and more than thirty thousand square meters of photovoltaic panels have been mounted. Although the panels are mostly sponsored by private individuals who produce energy that goes into the grid, the municipality has arranged that the systems owned by individuals can be installed for token rents on public roofs, such as schools, stadia, and parking garages, greatly reducing the negative visual impact of the systems. To promote the idea of the "solar region," the city sponsored the construction of a high-rise tower covered with solar panels at the train station and close by the construction of a three-story round tower devoted to storing and renting bicycles, which popularizes the city-wide system of bike paths. At the moment, bike travel accounts for one third of the transportation use in the city (Brandolini 2002).

Another important project for renewable sources of energy are eolian wind generators. After two generations, the cost/benefit analysis has improved 250 percent. The first significant wind farm of more than two hundred windmills was installed in California, at the Altmont Pass, during the energy crisis of the 1970s. Today, Denmark has primacy in the production and installation of eolic devices, satisfying twenty percent of the country's energy needs and producing about half of the world's windmills. Although the government provided incentives, the industries are cooperative and private and very competitive. The Middelgrunden Wind Farm, three miles off the coast of Copenhagen, was initiated in 2002 and creates an uncanny reef of two hundred–foot–high spinning towers. Germany, Holland, and Spain are particularly active in wind-generated energy; the region of Navarra, in northern Spain, where hundreds of windmills have been installed in green-belt areas, is close to achieving total energy autonomy. The sound pollution of windmills requires that they be distant from urban settings, positioned where there is maximum ventilation. They create a formidable fence and lend a territory, like the hills surrounding Pamplona, Spain, a new sense of urban limits.

Even if the attempts to steer cities toward sustainability during the last two decades have been numerous, alternative energy has not yet reached a critical mass, capable of changing the systems of the industrialized world. The power of petrol is deeply rooted in the world economy, too often to the discouragement of alternative resources. Automobile-based sprawl continues, with little opposition or bad conscience, in the name of the fluidity of consumerism.

Pamplona, wind farm park, 1990s.

Toward Agri-Civism

To heal the biosphere, the most urgent strategy should be the restructuring of urban systems, following the good examples of Portland, Curitiba, and Freiburg, the encouraging of living arrangements like BedZED, the investing in the creation of renewable energy sources, such as photovoltaics, wind, and hydrogen, the sponsoring of research on the creative reuse of refuse, and above all, the revising of transport systems in a manner that provides more sustainable options. One improvement that would be relatively easy to implement and could improve urban environmental quality with important social ramifications is the insertion of agriculture into urban situations.

Until a hundred years ago, the medium-size cities of Europe, cities of fewer than a hundred thousand inhabitants, maintained a clear visual order of built fabric and agricultural landscape. The equilibrium of medieval nucleus and cultivated fields was essential to the basic figure and ground reading of the cityscape. The role of agriculture in sustaining the city was clear in Ambrogio Lorenzetti's fresco depicting the city of Good Government in the town hall of Siena (1342). The productive landscape was isometric with the walled city. Today, more than ever, the agricultural terrain at the edge of cities has been compromised and put at risk. Suburbs have literally eaten the orchards. Land has more value for settlement than for food production. Planning studies always dictate in handsome colors "green areas" that are on closer inspection rarely green, and more likely paved and full of cars. With the onslaught of global warming, a question as complex as the environmental crisis cannot, of course, be solved by a simple return to urban agriculture. The participation of citizens in agricultural activities is among many things that can be easily achieved to influence the urban discourse toward ecological consciousness.

Without falling back on a nostalgia for the lost city, I would like to outline a tactic that could help change the current orientation of the urban system. The insistence on urban agriculture can be given the categorical name "agri-civism." The term derives from the very successful practice of agri-tourism, introduced in the 1980s in the farming lands of Italy, where hospitality functions helped to support the economy of working farms and thus to conserve the agricultural landscape. The urban version, which would involve the participation of self-motivated urban farmers and gardeners, would have a different social meaning, tied to the conservation of civic relationships. The so-called green spaces in non-central districts of cities are no-man's-lands, and there is a palpable feeling of danger. The presence of urban farmers would give green spaces a better sense of surveillance and guarantee the presence of citizens who have a proprietary tie to the land. Agri-civism would not necessarily be aimed at occasional visitors or tourists, but tied to the constant civic need for education, recreation, and the maintenance of greenery. Agri-tourism in Tuscany and Umbria has helped maintain the rural landscape heritage, and even when the category has been abused, it has encouraged the respect of farm lands, terraced orchards, and woods. By crossing the times and needs of tourism with agriculture, the rural landscape and its way of life have been saved from both agribusiness and abandonment.

Agri-tourism, Tuscany, 1990s.

Agri-civism would be an analogous attempt to cross agricultural activities with urban life. At present, European cities are more careful about urban development: the agricultural lands at the edge of cities and the brownfield ex-industrial sites have been studied for comprehensive urban requalification. Formalized by law in Italy in 1985, agri-tourism specified that no more than thirty percent of a farm's proceeds can derive from hotel functions. Within the order of city planning, a new law for agri-civism might demand a similar quota: at least thirty percent of any large site considered for renewal should be declared available for cultivation, rented to citizens for token annual fees.

The objectives of such an agenda are twofold: 1) to promote the synergy of built fabric and restored ecosystem; and 2) to establish a sense of belonging to and responsibility for urban space. Among the many precedents for such a policy are the laws for *orticelli di guerra,* published in the first years of World War II in Italy. The laws allowed citizens to cultivate victory gardens on all available lots, gardens, and empty spaces with the payment of token fees. Only the historic gardens were exempt from consideration. Even the Piazza del Duomo, the principal civic space of Milan, was planted with grain to dramatize the idea of victory gardens. While the current historic moment may not seem to require such urgency (despite the doubling of produce prices), the environmental crisis is in fact much more urgent than the threat of war. The plots for workers' gardens seen all over the train lines of France, Belgium, and Germany are signs of how many people desire to participate in urban agriculture. The city of Fano, Italy, for instance, has a program of 110 orchards, bordering on the autostrada, rented for nominal fees to elderly gardeners. If this voluntary labor could be directed toward more urban contexts, it would change the look and social composition of green spaces. In Ivry, a city on the edge of Paris, the fortress has been surrounded by six hundred small gardens to create a marvelous urban park. Even the metropolitan intervention of Euralille, composed of plinth, high-rises, and large covered spaces, is adjacent to an exemplary "children's farm," where students can come to observe farm animals.

Some examples of agri-civism may be found in the most unlikely places. In the heart of Lower Manhattan along Houston Street, there are two exceptional gardens that greatly contrast with the dense, unnatural fabric of New York: the *Time Garden*, a conceptual project by artist Alan Sonfist (1978) and the Liz Christie Community Garden (1972), cultivated by neighborhood volunteers. The first is a work of Land Art in which a typical New York lot, twenty-five by one hundred feet, has been fenced off, planted with indigenous species, and left purposely untended to return to a state of wilderness. The latter garden, run by a committee of local residents, is a horticultural information center and an example of how to recuperate abandoned urban lots. It inspired the reclamations of about six hundred brownfield sites in the New York area during the 1980s, often with the motivated guidance of the Green Guerillas. In East New York, an area chronically plagued by drugs, violence, and urban strife, a program was begun to reclaim sixteen percent of the abandoned sites and transform them into farming orchards. The activities of the resulting organization, East New York Farms! led to the foundation of two hundred orchards, averaging 250 square feet, worked by students ten to fourteen years old who are apprenticed to a knowledgeable gardener and paid a minimal fee for putting in a few hours of labor two days a week. The program led to more gardens and the creation of a weekly farmers market to sell the produce, averaging fifty to two hundred dollars in profits per week. The neighborhood is slowly changing into a more stable place: the neighbors participate more, and the young people learn about plant life and food, as well as about improving their diets.

In Italy in 1986, a brilliant idea, took root as a means of resisting the cultural and environmental degradation caused by fast food. Founded by Carlo Petrini at Bra in northern Italy, the Slow Food movement subscribes to a hedonistic form of activism. By partaking in wonderful meals it engages in defending genuine foods and local ways of cooking that are threatened with extinction. This alternative way of eating and cooking, which is superior from the standpoint of sustainability, health, and culture, represents a subversion of consumerism. Locally, the members of Slow Food participate in dining club, or *convivia*, that provide information about authentic foods that belong to a local genetic heritage. This conscientious defense of authentic food and the way it is grown in its territory provide a model for fighting against the standardizing forces of globalization, in the spirit of pleasure as one tastes local products. In recent years, Slow Food has advanced to the level of Slow Cities, for which a team of experts judges the local environmental quality and use of resources. Slow Food is a decidedly different approach to ecological consciousness than the guilt-trip strategies; the only guilt it may generate is from overeating.

The various exponents of the Social Forum inspired by Porto Alegre have organized equally optimistic efforts, often in league with Slow Food. A collective in Arezzo, Italy, known as the Fabbrica del Sole, has assembled a program of activities that will assist a hypothetical transition to bioregionalism. While they have offices in the center city, they also manage a farm and a Slow Food *convivium* in the countryside. Its first priority has been organizing a system for recycling organic refuse from restaurants and markets

The Edible School Yard, Martin Luther King School, Berkeley, 2002.
Naerum Citizen Gardens by C. Th. Sorensen, Copenhagen, 1950s.

as compost. A campaign has been organized for local planters to employ sheets of Mater-Bi, a biodegradable plastic made of corn starch, instead of the normal plastic coverings used to protect plants from weeds. For the local industries, the collective has introduced a system to furnish hydrogen as a renewable source of energy. And, for the local social questions, it has organized gatherings and celebrations to deal with problems in the neighborhoods. The idea of participatory democracy as it has been promoted at Porto Alegre and developed by various practitioners of the Social Forum agenda leads to a variety of concrete initiatives.

Agri-civism is not just a proposal for victory gardens, but also a way of encouraging civic participation. With a bit of imagination, kitchen-garden plots can become elements of a larger social network. In Denmark during the 1950s, C. Th. Sorensen designed an extraordinary park at Naerum, Havedonie, a suburb of Copenhagen. It represents the ideal to which agri-civism should aspire: a set of fifty private orchard plots, each contained within an elliptical hedge. Inside the hedges, the individual gardeners, who each have a small shed, grow whatever they desire—some roses, others vegetables— while outside the hedges, the landscape is publicly maintained as a high-quality park.

In Mexico City, at the Xochimilco Ecological Park by Raquel Elzondo and Mario Schjetnan (1990–95), there has been a similar attempt to blend the work of individuals with a public park. The initiative is part of the ecological recuperation of one of the five lakes of the valley of Mexico, all of which have almost completely dried up. The floating vegetable gardens of Xochimilco, a system used since the time of the Aztecs, are being revived as the lake waters are being replenished. Half of the park has been organized as a pleasure garden, while the other half is devoted to market stalls for selling plants. Small growers use the space to sell directly to the public.

Probably the largest attempt at realizing agri-civism is underway in the southern ranges of metropolitan Barcelona at the Agricultural Park of Baix Llobregat, a territory of several hundred square miles. An extensive area of periurban developments and industries mixed with agricultural lands and villages is in the process of being restructured as an immense park made of numerous sectors. Some of the initiatives are meant to halt the development of farm land being turned into housing sites: They have designated empty land as an arboretum to recuperate native plants. Parts of the regional park of Llobregat will be reshaped and terraced to prevent forest fires; and generally the landowners will be encouraged to continue to use the area for agriculture, but with the new possibility of public access. In designated areas, benches, fountains, and illumination have been installed. In others, bike paths connect spaces that were once separated by development. Reviving the terminology of the Garden City, the area is being shaped into an integrated green belt.

To intertwine cultivated land with urban fabric is a decorous way of increasing the local provision of foodstuffs and address the issues of hydraulic resources. The presence of agriculture in the city sets up a different sense of time and gears a place away from the daily routine to the cycles of the seasons. It creates a counterpoint to the fast pace of office jobs and traffic. The social impact of urban gardeners taking responsibility for urban sites may inspire a sense of belonging and place. Agriculture, which for centuries signified that which was not the city, can help an urban context acquire a renewed civic identity. It is just one of many meaningful changes needed to bring about a true synthesis of *sprawl* and *town*.

If "no smoking," why not "no greenhouse gas"? Xochimilco Ecological Park by Raquel Elzondo and Mario Schjetnan Mexico City, 1990–95.

Source List

Chapter I: Changing Weather

Alexander, Christopher et al. *A Pattern Language*. New York: Oxford University Press, 1978.

Banham, Reyner. *Los Angeles: The Architecture of Four Ecologies*. New York: Harper & Row, 1971.

Barthes, Roland. *Comment vivre ensemble: Simulations romanesques de quelques espaces quotidiens*. Edited by C. Coste. Paris: Editions du Seuil, 2002.

Bergson, Henri. *Creative Evolution*. Transcribed by Arthur Mitchell. New York: Henry Holt, 1911.

Boeri, S.; A. Lanzani; and E. Marini. *Il Territorio che cambia: Ambienti, paesaggi e immagini della regione Milanese*. Milan: Abitare Se gesta, 1993.

Chambless, Edgar. *Roadtown*. New York: Roadtown Press, 1910.

Choay, Francoise. *The Rule and the Model*. Cambridge, MA: MIT Press, 1997.

d'Andrea, L.; G. Quaranta; and G. Quinti. *Il ritorno della città: La base urbana della globalizzazione*. Rome: Officina Edizioni, 2000.

Deleuze, Gilles, and Felix Guattari. *A Thousand Plateaus: Capitalism and Schizophrenia*. Translated by B. Massumi. Minneapolis: University of Minnesota Press, 1987.

Godrei, Dinyar. *I cambiamenti climatici*. Rome: Carocci editore, 2003.

Krier, Leon. *Architecture: Choice or Fate?*. Windsor, UK: Andreas Papadakis, 1998.

Koolhaas, Rem. "Generic City." In *S,M,L,XL*. New York: Monacelli Press, 1994.

MVRDV. *Metacity Datatown*. Rotterdam: 010 Publishers, 1994.

La Cecla, Franco. *Perdersi: l'uomo senza ambiente*. Bari: Laterza, 1988.

Lerup, Lars. *After the City*. Cambridge, MA.: MIT Press, 2000.

Pope, Albert. *Ladders*. Houston: Rice University School of Architecture, 1996.

Picon, Antoine. *La ville territoire des cyborgs*. Besancon: Les Éditions de
  L'Imprimeuer, 1998.

Pynchon, Thomas. *The Crying of Lot 49*. New York : Vintage, 1966.

Sennett, Richard. *Flesh and Stone*. New York: Norton, 1998.

Turri, Eugenio. *La Megalopoli Padana*. Venice: Marsilio, 2000.

Vattimo, Gianni. *La società trasparente*. Milan: Garzanti, 1989.

Viganó, Paola. *La città elementare*. Milan: Skira, 2000.

Virilio, Paul. "La freccia del tempo." *Domus Dossier*, no. 4 (1996).

Virilio, Paul. *Ce qui arrive, naissance de la philofolie*. Paris: Editions Galilée, 2002.

Chapter II: Postcard City

Baudrillard, Jean. "Simulacra and Simulations." In *Jean Baudrillard: Selected Writings*.
  Edited by Mark Poster. Stanford, CA: Stanford University Press, 1998.

Blakely, E.J. and M.G. Snyder. "Divided We Fall. Gated and Walled Communities
  in the United States." In *Architecture of Fear*. Edited by Nan Ellin. New York:
  Princeton Architectural Press, 1997.

Bonomi, Aldo. *Il distretto del piacere*. Torino: Bollati Boringhieri, 2000.

Choay, Francoise. *L'Allégorie du Patrimoine*. Paris: Editions du Seuil, 1992.

Crick, Malcolm. "Representations of International Tourism in the Social Sciences: Sun,
  Sex, Sights, Savings, and Servility." *Annual Review of Anthropology* (1989).

Crawford, Margaret. "The World in a Shopping Mall." In *Variations on a Theme Park*.
  Edited by M. Sorkin. New York: Noonday Press, 1992.

Davis, R.C. and G.R. Marvin. *Venice: the Tourist Maze. A Cultural Critique of the
  World's Most Touristed City*. Berkeley, CA: University of California Press, 2004.

"Interview with Kenneth Frampton," *Design Book Review 8* (Winter 1986).

Judd, D.R. and S.S. Fainstein, eds. *The Tourist City*. New Haven: Yale
  University Press, 1999.

Gladwell, Malcolm. "Terazzo Jungle." *The New Yorker* (15 Mar. 2004).

Honey, Martha. *Ecotourism and Sustainable Development: Who Owns Paradise?*.
Washington DC: Island Press, 1999.

Koolhaas, Rem et al. *Harvard Design School Guide to Shopping*. Cologne, Germany:
Taschen, 2001.

Longstreth, Richard. *City Center to Regional Mall: Architecture, the Automobile, and
Retailing in Los Angeles, 1920-1950*. Cambridge, MA: MIT Press, 1997.

MacCannell, Dean. *The Tourist: A New Theory of the Leisure Class*. New York:
Schocken, 1976.

Nicholson-Lord, David. "The Politics of Travel: Is Tourism Just Colonialism in
Another Guise?." *The Nation* (6 Oct. 1997).

Pape, Robert A. "The strategic logic of suicide bombers." *International Herald
Tribune* (23 Sept. 2003).

Sontag, Susan. *On Photography*. New York: Anchor Books, 1977.

Stacchini, Valeria. "San Marino: Città-Stato, Città-Cartolina, Città-Lineare,
Città-Mercato... Città Normale." Thesis, Ferrara, 2003.

Smiley, David "History of the Victor: Constructing Shopping." *Lotus 118*
(Sept. 2003).

Chapter III: Jump-cut Urbanism

Bel Geddes, Norman. *Magic Motorways*. New York: Random House, 1940.

Barthes, Roland. *Mythologies*. Translated by A. Lavars. New York: Hill and Wang,
1957.

Berger, John. *Ways of Seeing*. London: Penguin, 1972.

Cohen, Jean-Louis. *Scenes of the World to Come: European Architecture and the
American Challenge, 1893-1960*. Paris: Flammarion, 1995.

de Certeau, Michel. *The Practice of Everyday Life*. Berkeley, CA: University of
California Press, 1984.

Dimendberg, Edward. "The Will to Motorization: Cinema, Highways, and
Modernity." *October 73* (Summer 1995).

Eisenstein, Sergei. *Film Form: Essays in Film Theory*. Edited and translated by Jay
    Leyda. New York: Harcourt Brace, 1949.

Fishman, Robert. *Bourgeois Utopias*. New York: Basic Books, 1987.

Flink, James. *The Car Culture*. Cambridge, MA: MIT Press, 1975.

Foster, Mark. *From Streetcar to Superhighway: American City Planners and Urban
    Transportation, 1900-1940*. Philadelphia: Temple University Press, 1981.

Garreau, Joel. *Edge City, Life on the New Frontier*. New York: Anchor Books, 1991.

Jackson, Kenneth. *Crabgrass Frontiers,The Suburbanization of the United States*.
    New York: Oxford University Press, 1985.

Kihlstedt, Folke T. "Utopia Realized: The World's Fairs of the 1930s." In *Imagining
    Tomorrow: History, Technology, and the American Future*. Edited by Joseph J.
    Corn, Cambridge, MA: MIT Press, 1986.

Le Corbusier. *La Ville Radieuse*. Paris: éditions d'Architecture d'Aujourd'hui, 1935.

Menduni, Enrico. *L'Autostrada del Sole*. Bologna: Il Mulino, 1999.

Michelson, Annette ed. *Kino-eye: the Writings of Dziga Vertov*. Berkeley, CA:
    University of California Press, 1984.

Mumford, Lewis. *The Highway and the City*. New York: Harvest Book, 1963.

Olmo, Carlo ed. *Il Lingotto 1915-1939: L'architettura, l'immagine, il lavoro*. Torino,
    Italy: Umberto Allemandi & co, 1994.

Venturi, Robert; Denise Scott Brown; and Steven Izenour. *Learning from Las Vegas*.
    Cambridge, MA: MIT Press, 1972.

Zardini, Mirko. *Asfalto*. Milano: Skira, 2003.

Chapter IV: Infrastructure as Art

Banham, Reyner. *Theory and Design in the First Machine Age*. New York: Praeger,
    1960.

Baxandall, Michael. *Patterns of Intention*. Berkeley, CA: University of California
    Press, 1985.

Billington, David P. *The Tower and the Bridge: The New Art of Structural Engineering*. Princeton: Princeton University Press, 1983.

Bohigas, Oriol. *Reconstruccion de Barcelona*. Barcelona: MOPU, 1986.

Bois, Yves-Alain and Rosalind Krauss, eds. *Formless: A User's Guide*. New York: Zone Books, 1997.

Calvesi, Maurizio, et al. *Martinetti e il Futurismo*. Rome: Edizioni De Luca, 1994.

Carboni, Massimo. *Il sublime è ora: saggio sulle estetiche contemporanee*. Roma: Castelvecchi, 1993.

Camfield, William A. *Marcel Duchamp Fountain*. Houston: The Menil Collection, 1989.

Chambless, Edgar. *Roadtown*. New York: Roadtown Press, 1910.

Copley, Stephen and Peter Garside eds. *ThePolitics of the Picturesque: Literature, Landscape and Aesthetics since 1770*. Cambridge and New York: Cambridge University Press, 1994.

da Costa Meyer, Esther. *The Work of Antonio Sant'Elia*. New Haven, CT: Yale University Press, 1995.

Eggener, Keith. *Luis Barragán's Gardens of El Pedregal*. New York: Princeton Architectural Press, 2001.

Flam, Jack ed. *Robert Smithson: The Collected Writings*. Berkeley, CA: University of California Press, 1996.

Guardia, Manuel. *Barcelona: Memoria desde el cielo*. Barcelona: Ajuntamento de Barcelona, 2002.

Haiquan, Li ed. *Road Interchanges of Beijing*. Beijing: Beijing Press, 1996.

Holston, James. *The Modernist City: An Anthropological Critique of Brasília*. Chicago: University of Chicago Press, 1989.

Bonifacio, Pes and Tanino. *Gibellina dalla A alla Z*. Gibellina: Museo d'Arte Contemporanea, 2003.

Piranesi, Giovan Battista. *Diverse maniere d'adornare i camini ed ogni altra parte degli edifizi desunte dall'architettura egizia, etrusca, greca e romana*. Rome: 1769.

Smithson, Robert. "A Tour of the Monuments of Passaic." *ArtForum* (Dec. 1967).

von Moos, Stanislaus. *Le Corbusier: Elements of a Synthesis.* Cambridge, MA: MIT Press, 1979.

Weyergraf-Serra, Clara and Martha Buskirk. *The Destruction of Tilted Arc.* Cambridge, MA: MIT Press, 1990.

Zanco, Federica ed. *Luis Barragán: The Quiet Revolution.* Milano: Skira, 2001.

Chapter V: The Ecology Question

Bramwell, Anna. *Ecology in the 20th Century: A History.* New Haven, CT: Yale University Press, 1989.

Christianson, Gale E. *Greenhouse: The 200-year Story of Global Warming.* Vancouver, BC: Greystone Books, 1999.

Buchanan, Peter. *Ten Shades of Green.* New York: Architectural League of New York, 2003.

Calthorpe, Peter. *The Next American Metropolis: Ecology, Community and the American Dream.* New York: Princeton Architectural Press, 1993.

d'Andrea, L.; G. Quaranta; and G. Quinti. *Il ritorno della città: La base urbana della globalizzazione.* Rome: Officina Edizioni, 2000.

Duany, A.; E. Plater-Zyberk; and J. Speck. *Suburban Nation: The Rise of Sprawl and the Decline of the American Dream.* New York: North Point Press, 2000.

Fernández Galiano, Luis. *El fuego y la memoria: Sobre arquitectura y energia.* Madrid: Alianza Editorial, 1991.

Hall, Peter and Colin Ward. *Sociable Cities: The Legacy of Ebenezer Howard,* Chichester, England: Academy Press, 1998.

Hawken, Paul; Amory Lovins; and L. Hunter Lovins. *Natural Capitalism: Creating the Next Industrial Revolution.* Boston: Little Brown, 1999.

Ingersoll, Richard. "Second Nature: On the Social Bond of Ecology and Architecture." In *Reconstructing Architecture.* Edited by T. Dutton & L. H. Mann. Minneapolis: University of Minnesota Press, 1996.

Lomborg, Bjorn. *The Skeptical Environmentalist: Measuring the Real State of the World*. Cambridge: Cambridge University Press, 2001.

McKibben, Bill. *The End of Nature*. New York: Anchor Books, 1989.

Prodi, Romano. "On signing the Kyoto Protocol." *International Herald Tribune* (6 April 2001).

Rees, Martin. *Our Final Hour*. London: Basic Books, 2003.

Schumacher, E. F. *Small is Beautiful*. London: Random Century Ltd., 1974.

Sontag, Susan. *Illness as Metaphor*. New York: Anchor Books, 1978.

Welter, Volker. *Biopolis, Patrick Geddes and the City of Life*. Cambridge, MA: MIT Press, 2002.

Index